Vietnam Vintage
Antiques from Southeast Asia, 1900-1950
William C. Mitchell

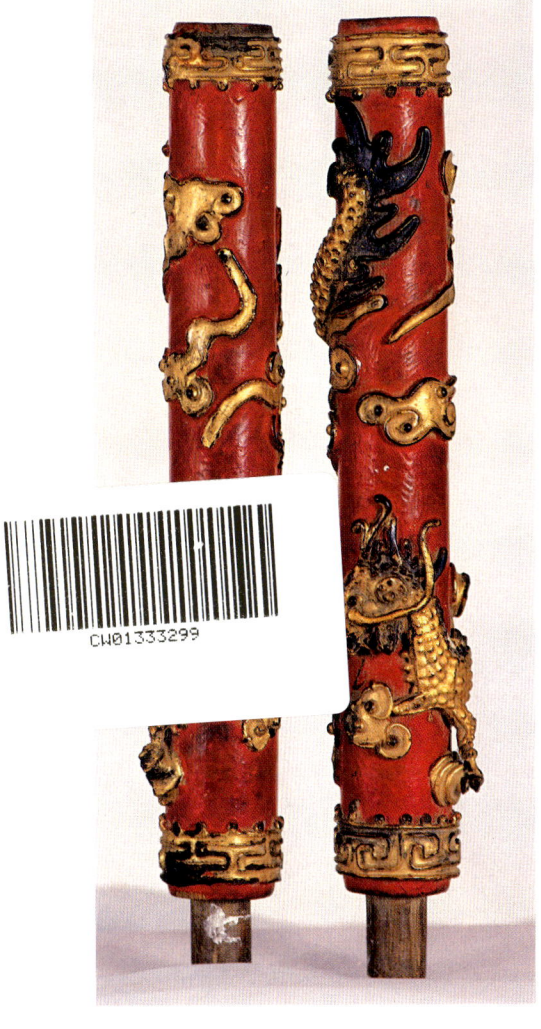

4880 Lower Valley Road, Atglen, PA 19310 USA

Copyright © 2004 by William C. Mitchell
Library of Congress Control Number: 2003110913

All rights reserved. No part of this work may be reproduced or used in any form or by any means—graphic, electronic, or mechanical, including photocopying or information storage and retrieval systems—without written permission from the publisher.

The scanning, uploading and distribution of this book or any part thereof via the Internet or via any other means without the permission of the publisher is illegal and punishable by law. Please purchase only authorized editions and do not participate in or encourage the electronic piracy of copyrighted materials.

"Schiffer," "Schiffer Publishing Ltd. & Design," and the "Design of pen and ink well" are registered trademarks of Schiffer Publishing Ltd.

Designed by Joseph M. Riggio Jr.
Type set in Exotic 350 DmBd BT/Korinna BT

ISBN: 0-7643-1958-2
Printed in China
1 2 3 4

Published by Schiffer Publishing Ltd.
4880 Lower Valley Road
Atglen, PA 19310
Phone: (610) 593-1777; Fax: (610) 593-2002
E-mail: Info@schifferbooks.com
Please visit our web site catalog at **www.schifferbooks.com**
We are always looking for people to write books on new and related subjects. If you have an idea for a book, please contact us at the above address.

This book may be purchased from the publisher.
Include $3.95 for shipping.
Please try your bookstore first.
You may write for a free catalog.

In Europe, Schiffer books are distributed by
Bushwood Books
6 Marksbury Avenue
Kew Gardens
Surrey TW9 4JF England
Phone: 44 (0) 20 8392 8585
Fax: 44 (0) 20 8392 9876
E-mail: Bushwd@aol.com
Free postage in the UK. Europe: air mail at cost.

Contents

Introduction: Themes and Context 4

Chapter 1: Lacquer 6

Chapter 2: Colors 22
    Red and Gold 22
    Blue and White 28

Chapter 3: The Animals of Supernatural Power 33
    Dragon 34
    Unicorn 40
    Phoenix 44
    Tortoise 48

Chapter 4: The Minor Animals 50

Chapter 5: Plants and Flora 59

Chapter 6: Objects 66

Chapter 7: Tea 71

Chapter 8: Habits 79
    Betel 79
    Tobacco 82

Chapter 9: Scholars 84

Chapter 10: The Chinese 96

Chapter 11: The Khmer 118

Chapter 12: The French 127

Chapter 13: Beliefs 131
    Ancestor Worship 131
    Buddhism 136
    Taoism 140
    Confucianism 147
    The Cao Dai 148
    Shamanism 148
    Christianity 152

Chapter 14: Times Change 154

Bibliography 160

Introduction
Themes and Context

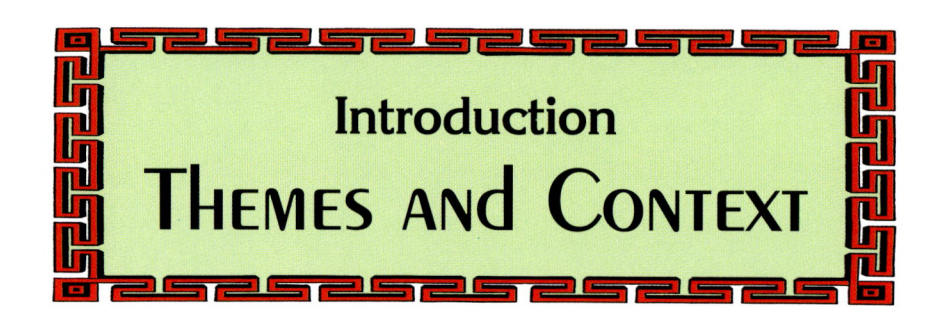

Putting this book together has been interesting, revealing, and fun. It has required a closer look at what has been collected and, in this case, it has raised two guiding questions. The first concerns what these items are but the more interesting question addresses the "whys" of the items and considers their meaning.

First, this is a collection of minor arts found in Vietnam. Many items available in Vietnam mirror this country's relationship with China, Cambodia, and France and are a part of this collection. For the moment, they are accessible and one would not need to go to a museum to find them. However, there has been a noticeable decline in numbers for some pieces and a few others have almost fallen from view. Of course these objects are for people to see but they should be handled and used rather than displayed and protected behind glass. Some are purely decorative but there is favor for pieces that can still have a practical use. The potential hands-on use of an old object is intriguing and has obviously influenced the decision to purchase.

There are a variety of materials like porcelain, metal, and cloth but this collection clearly leans towards lacquer ware and carvings from humble materials like pine, bamboo, and plywood. It includes many incised, relief, and openwork carvings. In each example the principal tool of the artist was a chisel and the irony of making something complex from something simple is much appreciated. Incised carvings are those in which artisans carve into the wood then fill in incisions with another material such as gold, silver, or mother of pearl. In relief carvings, artisans carve designs of varying depths into a piece of wood adding dimension to the overall work. Openwork carving is characterized by the entire removal of the ground so that one can see through the design. This collection has ample examples of each type and includes both complete pieces and fragments. Many of the panels, for example, were parts of cabinets, beds, or other larger pieces. The fragments exist independently as works of art in their own right and are aesthetically pleasing.

The "why" part of the process considers the intended use of an object. As can be expected, answers vary from person to person and different responses merely reflect how an object has been used. For example, a box originally made for the purpose of storing a particular item could be used for storing other objects. Or a tray intended for one purpose could easily find its way to another. Therefore, there can be disagreement over the particular use of this or that article. However, for items still found in temples or which retain their specialized purposes in ceremonies, there is general agreement.

There are items of a secular and religious nature. Secular pieces have a function in daily life activities like drinking tea or for special occasions like weddings. Religion and beliefs have played a dominant role in the creation of many of the works that are used in various ceremonies, rituals, and rites. Whether secular or religious, pieces are often adorned with common images and decorations meant to communicate certain themes and this leads to the more interesting aspect of the "why" issue.

In closely looking at these items, one comes to a better understanding of the meaning and the language of symbols. Many Vietnamese crafts are in great measure the offspring of temple and pagoda art. In style, content, and theme, they reflect Buddhist, Taoist, and Confucian influences. They also mirror traditional beliefs, for example, the place and importance of ancestors. To an important though less extent, Christianity has led to the creation of icons, altars, and other items that honor this imported faith but also reflect Vietnamese themes and sensibilities. There are religious figures, scenes from legends, plant life, real animals, and imaginary animals. All symbolize noble attributes or characteristics and well wishes such as longevity, good health, happiness, and wealth. These may appear with script to clearly express the idea behind a work while also serving a decorative function. There are objects such as scrolls and books that take on special meaning and enhance the well wish message of an article. There are stories and symbolism even in the choice of materials and colors. In general, several themes come together in a single piece and it is not always clear which establishes dominance. Common messages come through over a wide variety of items. As such, a tea tray can have the same information to convey as a piece of embroidery or a wall panel.

Symbolism and imagery, with deep roots in the relationship to China and the presence of the Chinese in Vietnam, dominate this art. The creators usually included a generally understood symbol language in their presentations. The collection reflects the strong presence of themes in Vietnamese life. Materials, colors, animals, mythical beasts, plant life, and special objects comprise the language. These works also shed light on customs, the importance of academic achievement, national struggle, religion, beliefs, and finally, change. For these reasons, this book is arranged according to particular themes and aspects of Vietnamese life as reflected in the work. As much as possible, items have been arranged according to type or function within these thematic sections. This seems logical and natural since most of the pieces, whatever their function, include common decorative motifs and, therefore, a common symbolic language. For the better part, these works are not art for art's sake. Rather, they derive from a specific context, are imbued with special meaning, and have a sense of purpose. Obviously, the artisan wanted the audience to appreciate creations for their functional and aesthetic value. But there was always the intent of the creator to speak to the observer. In the overwhelming majority of cases, the names of the artisans who created these beautiful objects are anonymous as work was rarely signed. Perhaps in their minds, the message and purpose of the item were of greater importance than the identity of the artisan. I hope that the reader will arrive at a general understanding of these pieces, their meaning, and their relationship to the people of Vietnam.

Chapter 1
LACQUER

Most of the wooden pieces in this collection are covered with several layers of lacquer. So lacquer is a good place to begin. The natural sap of the Rhus vernicifera tree, lacquer is the cornerstone of woodwork in Vietnam. The resin is collected from the tree by tapping in much the same manner as rubber is harvested. Its great advantage is versatility as it can be painted, carved, or inlaid. In addition, lacquer is highly resistant to damp, heat, and insects making it very practical and much appreciated in this tropical environment.

Knowledge of the artistic potential of lacquer came to Vietnam from China centuries ago and, over time, the Vietnamese have perfected its use. According to some sources, work in lacquer has its roots in the court of Emperor Le Nhan Ton (1443-1460) who sent a Mandarin of his Imperial Court to China, his mission to learn trades to be taught to local artisans to provide them with new economic resources and opportunities. The Mandarin returned several months later with a basic knowledge of Chinese lacquer work, but his new learning was sufficient only for waterproofing barges. Unfortunately, the King's envoy had not learned how to attach gold and silver designs into the wood in the manner of the Chinese. So he requested and received the King's permission to return to China. On this second journey, he learned these deeper secrets of the trade and returned with them to Vietnam.

Lacquer work is a time intensive process and it requires the attention and skills of a number of craftsmen. First, the craftsman must prepare the wood. At this initial stage, he treats the wood with a special coating then fills and sands it, a process lasting several weeks. A typical piece has ten coats of lacquer and workers must carefully dry each coat for a period of about one week. The dried coat is sanded to prepare it for the next coat of lacquer. And so it goes until the requisite number of coats are applied. Woods commonly used are plywood for smaller items and teak for larger pieces such as furniture. Common colors for the finished product are gold, red, cinnabar (a brilliant red derived from vermilion, the sulfide of mercury), brown, and black. Over the centuries, other items like gold, silver, and mother of pearl were used to color the lacquer. In modern times, producers have turned to chemicals to achieve this effect given considerations of time and expense.

Mother of pearl is typically used for inlay work and it is a process which is also time consuming and complicated. Mother of pearl work has a long and noble history in Vietnam with artisans from the village of Chuon Ngo in the northern province of Ha Tay of special note and reputation. The craft, which demands skillful hands, artistic eyes, and creative minds, has been passed along for generations. In the days of royalty, the artisans from this village produced tea trays inlaid with mother of pearl. These tea trays were found in royal courts and on the banquet tables of kings, queens, and lords. In those times, such articles were the reserve of the wealthy and they considered it noble and dignified to place mother of pearl work in strategic places in the home.

A round lacquer box for the wedding ceremony with a procession scene in mother of pearl inlay, c. 1900 (D 10.5", H 4"). $600.

Adding this substance to lacquer requires several steps. Prior to inlaying the chips, they must be designed, grinded, cut, carved, chiseled, and polished. Completed designs usually recall ancient tales, often of warriors and battles, and feature natural scenery with birds, butterflies, and flowers.

Artisans continue the craft and Vietnamese lacquer ware today has a world reputation for quality and craftsmanship. We are very fortunate that the Vietnamese took the use of lacquer beyond plugging up barges and have given us a unique and classic form of beauty to be appreciated in all manner of objects.

Cover detail of the procession of a nobleman and his wife on horseback led by two attendants who carry banners.

An unusual, miniature, and round lacquer wedding box with painted flowers and designs, c. 1920 (D 5.5", H 3"). $250.

Open view of the miniature wedding box.

Octagonal lacquer sweets box with nine trays and a cover painting of two noblemen and an attendant, c. 1920 (W 12", H 4"). $350.

8

An unusual, round and carved lady's powder box with a lacquer frame holding a porcelain receptacle, c. 1900 (D 4.2", H 1.5"). $450.

Detail of the porcelain dish with poem script and painted flowers.

A round, red lacquer betel box with painted floral and cloud motifs, c. 1920 (D 10", H 2"). $250.

Lady's jewelry box with mother of pearl inlay flowers and butterflies, symbols for joy and courtship, c. 1920 (6.5" x 3.8" x 3.5"). $350.

Lady's red lacquer make-up box with appliqué flowers, characters, and designs, c. 1920 (9" x 9" x 5.1"). $300.

Lady's accessory box with floral motif in mother of pearl inlay, c. 1920 (5.5" x 3.5" x 2.5"). $250.

Lady's make-up box with heavily stylized paintings of fabulous beasts along each side, c. 1900 (9" x 9" x 5"). $350.

Lady's accessory box with slide-up mirror, brass handle, and characters that promise a beautiful smile, c. 1940 (6.2" x 8.3" x 6"). $350.

A small accessory box for a lady, with stand-up mirror and two drawers, c. 1940 (6" x 7.5" x 5"). $200.

A red lacquer ladies dressing stand with a lamp in the form of a pavilion, c. 1940 (16" x 11" x 18.5"). $350.

A square lacquer storage box with painted designs, c. 1920 (16.5" x 16.5" x 8"). $300.

Detail of the painting of a penholder, a symbol for pursuit of knowledge in literature, science, and philosophy, and a sign of a scholar.

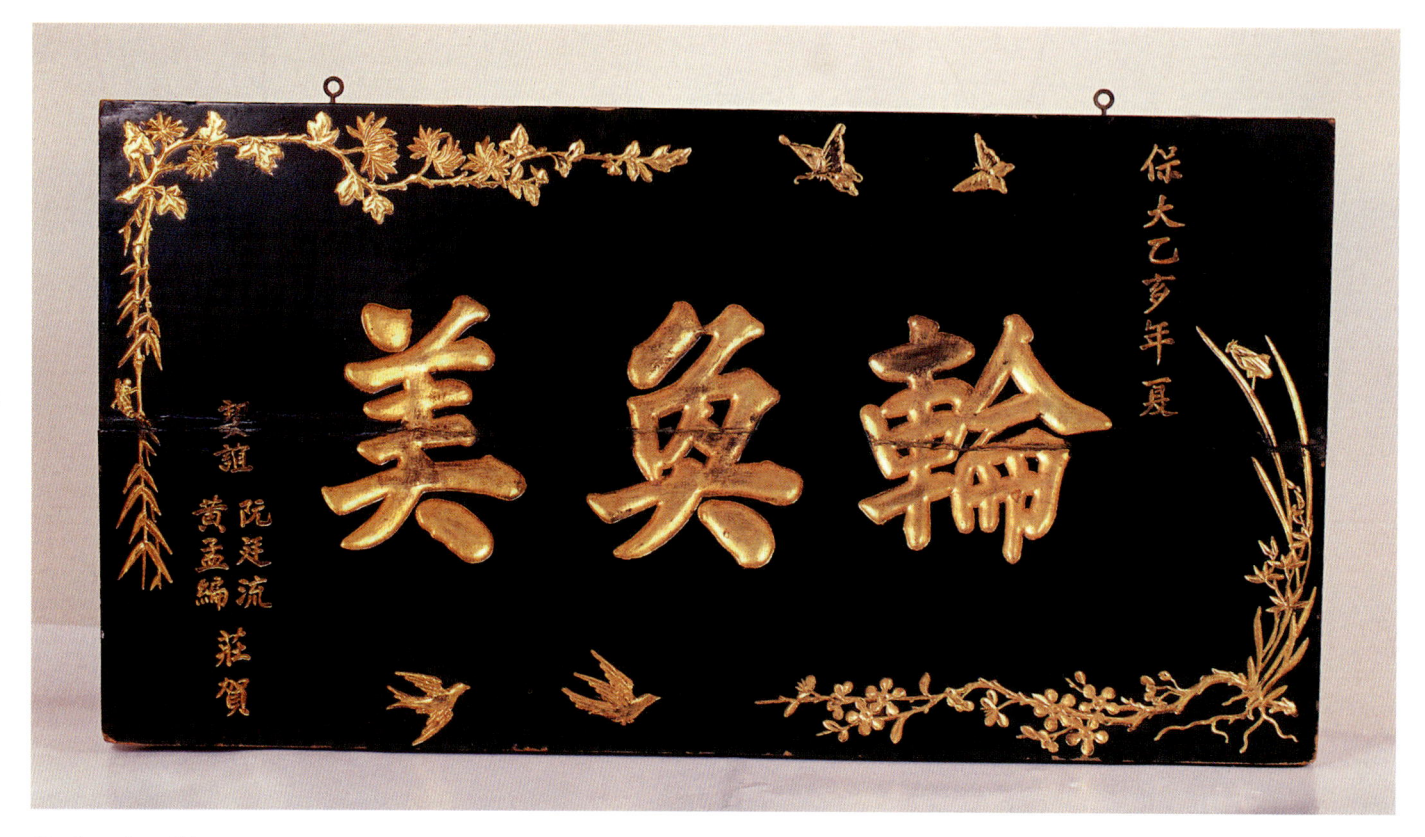

Black and gold lacquer well wish banner congratulating an official on a new home, given in the time of Emperor Bao Dai, c. 1940 (42" x 22"). $850.

A lacquer panel detailing the history of a pagoda, probably the gift of a local family, c. 1940 (31" x 19.5"). $350.

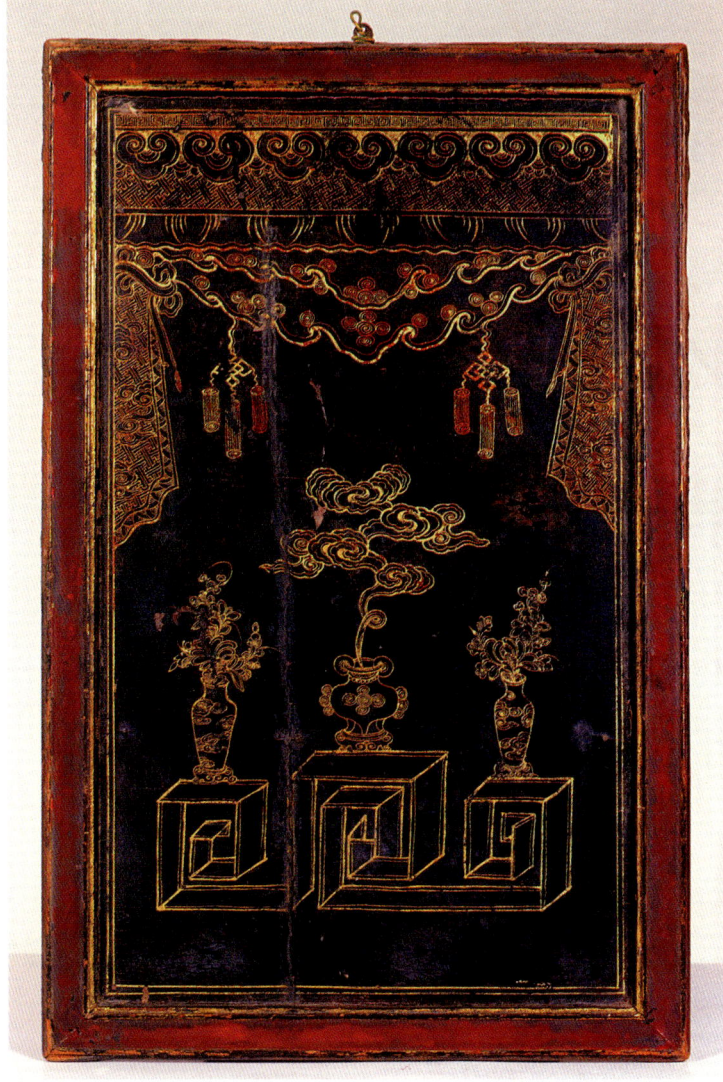

Lacquer painting of two flower vases and a perfume bottle exuding scented smoke, all atop an offering stand, c. 1920 (26.5" x 17"). $350.

Lacquer painting of the God of Longevity with his gourd containing the Elixir of Life, Deer with a longevity plant only it can locate, and Bats for fortune, c. 1940 (23.5" x 15.5"). $550.

Detail from a lacquer painting of a Buddhist monk holding an umbrella, symbol of purity, c. 1950.

Lacquer panel of two dignitaries on horseback and with attendants as they pass a lone fisherman by a bridge, c. 1920 (32" x 24.5"). $600.

Bone appliqué figures on lacquer of women and attendants. Below, "100 antiquities," a general collection of items with noble attributes, c. 1920 (31" x 11"). $350.

Detail of the procession.

A red lacquer offering stand with curved legs and carving of the face of Dragon emerging from stylized flora, c. 1920 (21" x 14.5" x 9"). $400.

A red lacquer offering stand with carved designs and curved legs, c. 1920 (13" x 8" x 8.5"). $350.

Red lacquer icon stand with curved legs, c. 1920 (16" x 13" x 6.5"). $250.

A portrait stand with mother of pearl inlay designs of birds and flowers, c. 1900 (17.5" x 5.8" x 22"). $600.

Gold lacquer window panel with floral carvings which converge at the top into Butterfly, a symbol for courtship and marital happiness, c. 1940 (25" x 20.5"). $400.

Detail of Butterfly.

A rack for ceremonial, wooden swords, floral designs carved in openwork, c. 1940 (15" x 10.5" x 9"). $250.

Detail of an openwork panel of a humming bird sipping nectar from a flower, c. 1920.

Chapter 2
Colors

Red and Gold

Certain colors in these pieces have a meaning and purpose and are a commentary on virtues and the expression of the wish for happiness, joy, and contentment. The principal color combinations one sees are red-gold and blue-white.

Red and gold are common colors for lacquered items and they appear regularly in other arts and crafts. These colors are so prominent because they mean luck, fortune, and happiness. Red, strongly linked to happiness, is seen everywhere during festival times like Lunar New Year. At this special time, banners and festive clothing are often red. Giving money is a custom at Lunar New Year and people offer monetary gifts enclosed in red packets. Red is also associated with blood, fire, and the sun. As such, it is the color for life itself. Gold has an obvious link to money and fortune. In addition to the wish for wealth and prosperity, it means good luck. Together, red and gold are linked with life, wealth, and nobility and they are an amplification of good tidings. It is no mystery that pagodas and holy places are filled with objects in these colors.

An unusual pair of octagonal, lacquer tops from wooden beams symbolizing the wind, c. 1920 (H 15.5"). $350/pair.

Detail of carved serpent Dragon.

An unusual, red and square lacquer wedding box with handle in the form of a flower, c. 1940 (10" x 9.5" x 9.5"). $450.

A round and tiered bamboo food box with gold colored designs and a harvest scene, c. 1900 (D 10", H 13.5"). $600.

Detail of a boy riding Water Buffalo, a symbol for good harvest and springtime, and villagers who carry harvest implements.

A leather storage chest with gilt figures of birds and flora enclosed in an interlocking line design, c. 1900 (26" x 12" x 11.5"). $750.

An unusual ancestor stand with relief figures of a couple reading from tablets, c. 1900 (14" x 8.5"). $400.

Fragment from a gilt temple banner, possibly used to keep incense, c. 1940 (8.5" x 2" x 10"). $150.

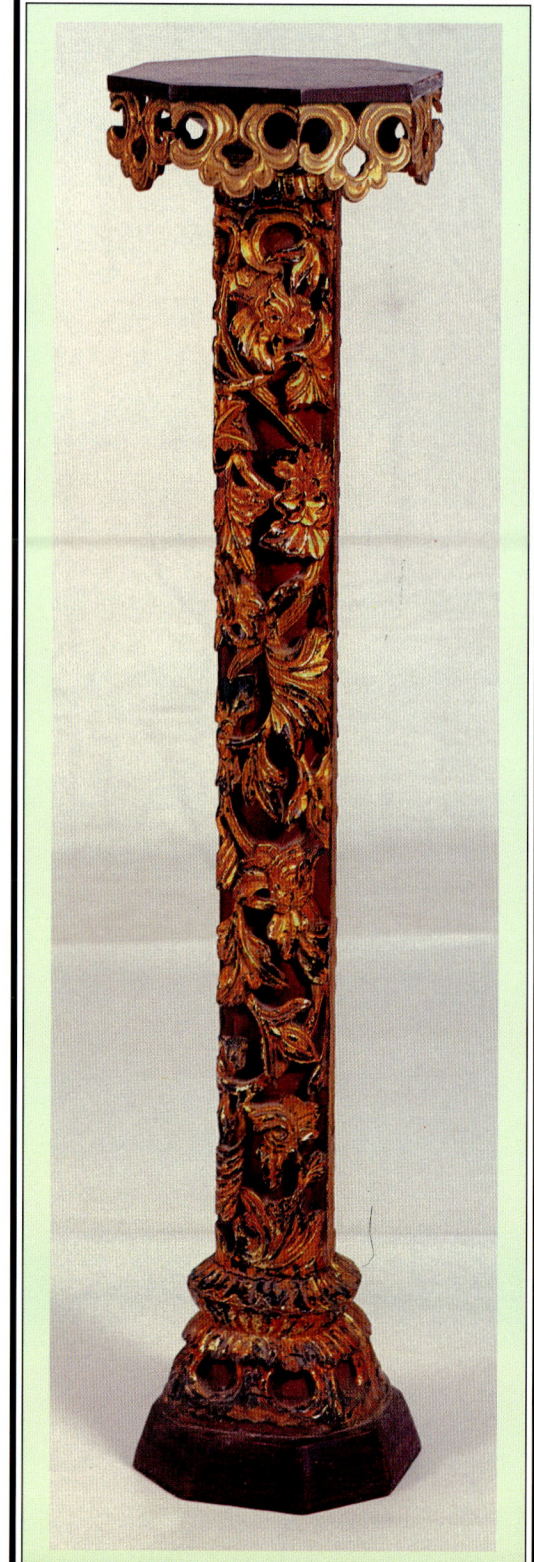

A candle stand for the altar encircled by relief carvings of stylized flowers, c. 1940 (H 36.5"). $550.

A wooden stand to support a plate of offerings to spirits, supports in the form of the face of Dragon, c. 1940 (H 5"). $250.

A pair of wooden scepters for display to convey well wishes, c. 1900 (L 19"). $250/pair.

A hall mirror with carved and painted designs, c. 1940 (34" x 23.5"). $400.

Blue and White

The other predominant color combination, blue and white, is typical for porcelain items. Similarly, these colors are meaningful. White is a sign for a mild mood and of moral purity. Blue recalls the sky and suggests the celestial. It has been said that in using blue for porcelain, artisans were attempting to capture the blue of the sky following rain. Together these colors mean contentment and goodness.

Porcelain sheets in a wood frame with painted scenes of villagers flanked by protective Dragons Among Clouds, c. 1900 (10" x 20"). $450.

Detail of friends on a stroll, a scene from village life.

Porcelain sheets in a wood panel with paintings of a pavilion, a horseman, friends, and a landscape, c. 1940 (36" x 10"). $700/pair.

Detail of a gathering of friends.

A water jar painted with the God of Longevity and attendants and with inscriptions for fortune and long life, c. 1950 (D 10", H 11.5"). $350.

On this panel, scenes of noblemen, village life, and landscapes.

Underside of a porcelain rice bowl with painted scene of companions beneath pine, for steadfast friendship, c. 1920 (D 6.5", H 3"). $200.

Porcelain pillow with a painting of a stylized bee, for industry and order, and a peony flower, for spring and feminine beauty, c. 1920 (6" x 4.5" x 3"). $150.

An unusual pair of porcelain candle holders in the form of reclining Happy Buddhas, c. 1920 (L 3", H 2"). $350/pair.

A pair of ceramic accessory jars for a lady, c. 1940 (D 2.5", H 3.9"). $200/pair.

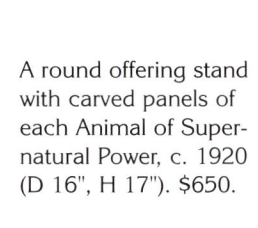

Chapter 3
The Animals of Supernatural Power

In the Vietnamese cosmos roam The Four Animals of Extraordinary and Supernatural Power. Each is firmly affixed in the national consciousness. They make up the national Coat of Arms, represent traditional Vietnamese values, and have special meaning. In order of power and importance, they are Dragon, Unicorn, Phoenix, and Tortoise.

Each plays a decisive role in spiritual and secular matters. This is especially true of Dragon whose image is most often seen day to day and during ceremonies and festivals. Each has special powers and spheres of influence. While their areas of power sometimes overlap, there are distinctive characteristics.

We find them with amazing regularity in all artistic mediums, often portrayed against a background of natural surroundings from which they emerge in transformation. This ability suggests that all life is interconnected and renewed through metamorphosis and transformation. An understanding of the meaning of each of these creatures is central to an appreciation of the arts and crafts of Vietnam. One could argue that their presence and the meaning they imbue in a piece are of no less importance than the function of that article.

The mythical nature of three of these animals, Dragon, Phoenix, and Unicorn, accounts at least in part for differences in how artists render them. Variations also arise from the fact that, except for Tortoise, these animals are composites of other, real animals. This leaves quite a bit of room for individual imaginations. There is little discord in the portrayal of Tortoise, which, after all, is real. But while artists and craftsmen may interpret physical appearances differently, the distinctive symbolism of each creature remains constant. All embody noble qualities and their presence is the expression for good luck and fortune.

A round offering stand with carved panels of each Animal of Supernatural Power, c. 1920 (D 16", H 17"). $650.

Dragon

Among the Animals of Supernatural Power, Dragon, a strong male figure, rules. He is most often portrayed and when seen with the other animals, Dragon is usually most prominent. He is of special significance to Vietnamese as according to legend, the Vietnamese people descended from a Dragon line.

A carved panel of a horned Dragon in transformation.

Lacquer panel of the face of Dragon (look closely to find it) and stylized Bats in each corner, c. 1920 (10" x 7"). $150.

According to the tale, King Lac Long Quan (Dragon Lord) of the legendary Hong Bang Dynasty (2879 BC-258 BC), to whom the Vietnamese trace their ancestry, was a descendent of Dragons and the grandson of The God of the Seas. He married Au Co, a descendent of the Angels of the Mountains and their union produced one hundred sons, the eggs carried in a pouch by Au Co. All of these sons would grow into handsome and healthy men. As time went on the King and his wife experienced discord in their marriage and decided to part, each taking fifty sons.

King Lac Long Quan took his fifty sons to live with him on the sea and fifty went with their mother, Au Co, to live in the mountains. The couple did not meet again until the sons became men. Upon meeting, Au Co said to King Lac Long Quan, "You left me alone with our sons and I am living like a widow." The King replied, "Although our children came from the joining of sea and land, we are like yin and yang, opposites like water and fire, and we are not meant for each other." They parted never to meet again. The eldest son founded the first dynasty under the name Hung Vuong. And so goes the legend.

Dragon is a combination of a host of real animals. He has the antlers of a deer, eyes of a fish, ears of a buffalo, body and neck of a snake, scales of a carp, claws of an eagle, and feet of a tiger. The tail is usually coiled. The protuberance of his head is an indication of his great wisdom and intelligence. In carefully crafted Dragons, the crest has eighty-one scales running the length of the backbone. Through flared nostrils, Dragon breathes a special kind of smoke that he can transform at will into fire or water.

Dragon was the symbol of the Emperor and in imperial times the number of claws on the figure of Dragon indicated rank. The five-clawed Dragon signaled royalty and implements so adorned were for the exclusive use of the King. Four-clawed Dragons were reserved for high dignitaries of the Royal Court, the appropriate number of claws found on their clothing as markings of rank. The more common three-clawed Dragon indicated lower rank.

Dragon is an omnipotent figure and as the master of earth, sea, and sky, he moves freely and powerfully through all. His image connotes valor, heroism, and power, both royal and personal. Dragon's power over personal lives is quite complete and impressive, and seems to last for eternity. For the living, Dragon influences happiness, wealth, and prosperity. For the dead, he determines peace.

An openwork panel of a long-maned Dragon emerging from flora, c. 1920 (4.5" x 11"). $300.

A gold lacquer standing and coiled Dragon, fragment from an altar, c. 1900 (H 7"). $200.

An incense stand encircled with carving of Dragon emerging from flora, c. 1920 (H 29"). $400.

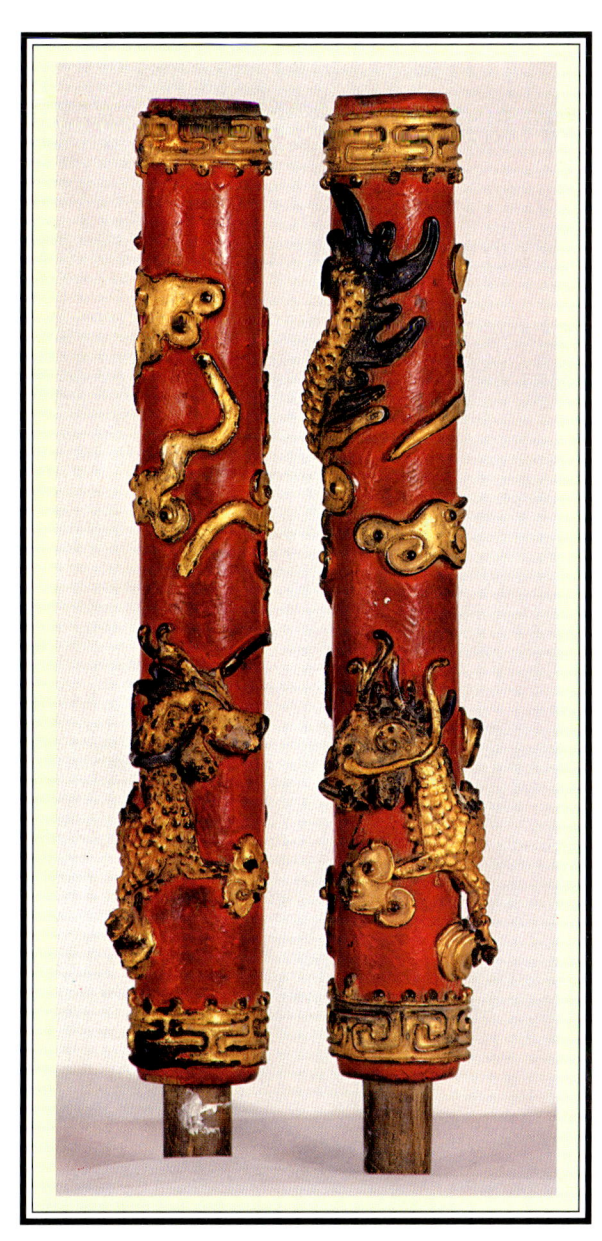

A pair of altar candle stands, each encircled by a carving of Dragon coiled to form the confronting posture, c. 1920 (D 2", H 15"). $500/pair.

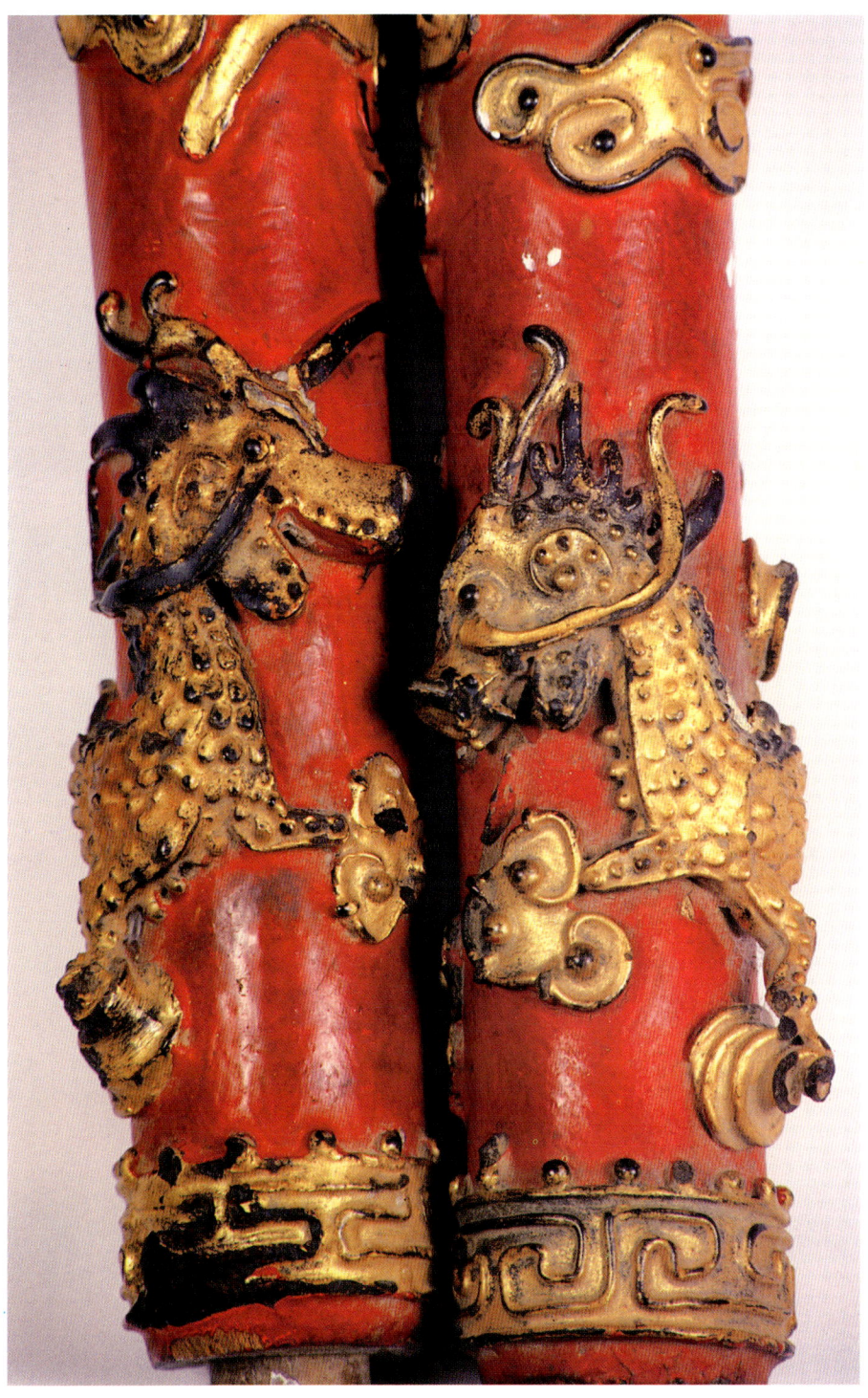

Detail of confronting Dragons.

A lacquer altar stand, probably for an icon, with carvings of serpent Dragons at each side, c. 1940 (8" x 8" x 3"). $200.

Detail of serpent Dragons.

Rectangular lacquer box with serpent Dragon transformation motif in mother of pearl inlay, c. 1900 (9" x 4.5" x 5"). $450.

38

An unusual icon stand with curved legs, painted and carved with Dragon motifs, c. 1900 (15" x 9.5" x 3.5"). $400.

Detail of opposite side features the carved and gilt face of Dragon.

Unicorn

Unicorn is second in the hierarchy and brings about the widest variations in artists' interpretations of its image. Consequently, there can be much dispute about what is or is not Unicorn. Complicating matters further, Unicorn has a range of reference terms including "Licorne," "Kylin," "Horse Dragon," and even "Lion." However, the term "Unicorn" is most common among shop owners and it seems to be the most popular term of reference among Vietnamese in general. Therefore, in this book "Unicorn" will be used.

A carved panel of Unicorn in transformation.

Openwork panel of Unicorn in the forest, c. 1940 (8" x 7.5"). $200.

Unicorn has hoofs, fishlike scales, and its tail is usually coiled in three or five flames. Each flame represents one of the five elements (gold, wood, water, fire, and earth) and, in turn, each element has its own virtues.

Unicorn's appearance is powerful and warlike but its distinctive characteristics are kindness and benevolence. A gentle beast, Unicorn bears no ill will and would not harm an insect or the grass under its feet. It has a pleasant sounding voice like bells and other musical instruments and can walk on land or water. It only appears on auspicious occasions. It is rumored that the birth and death of Confucius were two such times.

Unicorn is connected to royalty and its steps symbolize genealogy of an imperial family. Unicorn is also of special importance to those who rule because it knows when wise and great leaders will appear on earth. This quality makes Unicorn a sign and symbol for wise administration, good government, and benevolent leadership.

Its image is a good omen and when seen at wedding ceremonies, it is a wish for numerous children and good fortune. Unicorn is also a symbol of the strength of deities and has power over evil spirits and ghosts. In carvings, this animal often bears The Sacred Text upon its back, a symbol of the pursuit of academic excellence, especially in literature and science. Alternatively, the books on the Unicorn can symbolize the Book of the Law. All in all, Unicorn's presence is the sign for perfect goodwill, gentleness, and kindness to all living creatures.

Openwork panel of Unicorn and a bird overhead, c. 1940 (10" x 10.5"). $200.

A pair of gold lacquer Unicorns roam in opposite directions, c. 1940 (6" x 10"). $250.

Panel of fierce looking Unicorn between a nobleman reading a sacred scroll and an attendant, all with black eyes, c. 1900 (6" x 15"). $200.

Panel of majestic Unicorn sailing on clouds, its flaming tail a symbol of the spirit of fire, heat, power, and authority, c. 1920 (9.5" x 4.5"). $150.

Detail from an embroidery on silk of Unicorn among clouds with The Sacred Text upon its back as magic smoke issues from its mouth, c. 1920.

Phoenix

Phoenix is the counterpart of Dragon and a feminine sign. In times past her image adorned items to be used by women. This remarkable, powerful, and graceful bird embodies all good virtues as she reigns over sky and water. She stands on the waves of the sea and bathes her wings, which possess great power and represent the wind itself. In flight the feathers, made up of the five fundamental colors, light up in flames and the wings produce a metallic sound. The song of Phoenix is one of great beauty and it includes the five notes of the traditional music scale.

Carved panel of Phoenix emerging in transformation from flora.

A ceremonial wooden sword with carved designs along the length of blade and the handle in the form of Phoenix, c. 1940 (L 32"). $350.

Phoenix has the skin of a serpent, forehead of a swallow, back of a tortoise, neck of a snake, and tail of a fish. With her head a symbol of the sky, her eyes the sun, her back the moon, her feet the earth, and her tail the planets, Phoenix represents the universe and possesses all of its power, force, and beauty. Phoenix is, therefore, well equipped for the role as overseer of warmth and harvest.

Phoenix is a bird of mystery and mere mortals will have great difficulty witnessing her presence for Phoenix keeps out of view in times of peace and hides herself in times of war and tribulation. She seeks a world where reason prevails, an attribute making Phoenix a symbol and gauge of peace. When Phoenix appears in the arts, she often has The Sacred Scroll suspended from her beak extending her symbolism to include the power of learning and knowledge.

Detail of the Phoenix-shaped handle.

Panel of an Immortal holding a lotus flower and upon the back of Phoenix, The Scroll suspended from her beak, c. 1920 (24" x 9"). $350.

A porcelain rice bowl with a painting of Phoenix in flight, c. 1950 (D 4.5", H 2.4"). $150.

Jewelry box with a stand-up frame topped by two Phoenixes that soar in opposite directions, c. 1900 (12" x 12" x 18.8" frame up). $650.

Tortoise

Finally, there is humble Tortoise who occupies the fourth position among the Animals of Supernatural Power. Above all, Tortoise is a symbol of longevity, strength, and endurance. Its inclusion in this exclusive club is probably linked to its round and level shell. In ancient times, fortune-tellers used the shell in holy rites to divine future events. Soothsayers tossed the shell upon live coals and future events were revealed to them in the sounds of the shell as it popped and exploded from the heat.

A carved panel of Tortoise emerging from lotus flowers.

Panel of an Immortal holding a gourd containing the Elixir of Life and on the back of Tortoise, symbol of longevity, c. 1920 (24" x 9"). $350.

The dome-shaped shell of Tortoise symbolizes heaven and earth. The shell itself suggests the vault of heaven, while the square plaque at its underside represents the surface of the earth. In carvings, Tortoise may support Sacred Crane enhancing the theme of longevity. Tortoise is said to live for ten thousand years while Crane lives for one thousand years. Seen together, the meaning is expressed by the well wish, "May you be remembered for one thousand years, and may your cult endure for ten thousand years." Tortoise is often rendered with The Sacred Text upon its back. One explanation holds that this is a text about the story of the invention of a diagram representing the division of the universe into male and female principles. The diagram is said to be the creation of Emperor Dai Vu (2205-2197 BC) and resulted from his study of the shell of Sacred Tortoise.

Bronze incense burner in the form of fierce Warrior Tortoise, c. 1920 (H 10"). $350.

Chapter 4
The Minor Animals

In addition to the Animals of Supernatural Power, there are creatures of second rank. The fact that they are real makes them somewhat less mystical than their supernatural brethren, but, similarly, all have special powers and attributes. Most commonly seen in this group are Bat and Lion. Other minor animals are Elephant, Tiger, Rat, and Fish.

An ancestor banner in the form of Bat, for placement over the family altar, c. 1940 (6" x 8.5"). $150.

Panel of stylized and gilt Bat with suspended tassels, symbol of congratulations, and poem script on fortune and the virtues of goodness, c. 1920 (26.5" x 19") $650.

Overall, Bat is a symbol for happiness. When five appear together, it is a symbol for the "Five Happinesses." These are riches, peace, health, love of virtue, and a natural death at an advanced age. Flowers suspended from Bat's mouth enhance the happiness motif.

A wall panel in the form of Bat inscribed with a happiness wish, c. 1920 (9" x 14"). $150.

Detail of Deer in the forest, perhaps in search of the longevity plant.

A wooden banner in form of Bat with appliqué figures of Deer, trees, and flora, c. 1920 (19.5" x 28.5"). $650.

51

Lion figures in Buddhism as the defender of law and the protector of sacred buildings and is generally rendered with a fierce appearance. Artists also portray Lion as playing with a ball held snugly under its paw. The ball may symbolize the sun, natural power, a precious stone, or a sacred sphere. Some legends have it that Lion can produce milk from its paws and that in ancient times, provincial people left hollow balls in places where Lion could find and play with them. They did this with the hope that some milk from Lion would find its way into the ball. They would retrieve the ball later and enjoy this special milk.

Red and gold lacquer Guardian Lions, remains of a temple altar, c. 1900 (H 8.5"). $350/pair.

Candle stand in form of Lion who holds a ball or sacred sphere snugly under its foot, c. 1900 (3.5" x 7" x 5"). $350.

Candle stand in form of Lion with a ball or sacred sphere under its foot, c. 1900 (3.5 x 8.5 x 10.5"). $350.

Embroidery on silk of Lion at play with her cubs as Bats with peaches, for immortality and spring, fly above, c. 1900 (37" x 25"). $900.

Detail from embroidery on silk of a green-eyed Lion above a fabulous bird with floral patterns between them.

54

Elephant is a symbol of strength, energy, and prudence. Elephant too has a special place in Buddhism and is often depicted offering flowers or water to Buddha. Elephant is a frequent steed for holy men and its association with prudence brings Elephant into special favor with rulers.

A pair of ceramic oil lamps in the form of Sacred White Elephants, c. 1920 (2.5" x 4" x 7"). $500/pair.

A blue and white ceramic ewer in the form of Elephant and with the face of Dragon at the saddle, c. 1920 (2" x 3.5" x 5.5"). $300.

A bronze candle stand for the altar in the form of red-eyed Warrior Elephant, c. 1940 (H 9"). $450.

The image of Tiger signals the dignity and sternness of leaders as well as the special courage and fierceness prized in a warrior. It seems that demons and evil spirits have a special fear of Tiger and its presence, especially at the entrance of temples, is meant to frighten bad spirits and drive them away.

A gold lacquer guardian Tiger with black stripes and circular eyes of carved bone, c. 1940 (4.8" x 8.5") $150.

Detail of taming the tiger.

Oil painting recounting the legend of taming the tiger, a means for mortals to attain special powers, c. 1950 (28 x 38 in). $700.

Rat on the one hand is a symbol of timidity and meanness, but on the other, Rat is resourceful and can locate and maintain a large food supply. Because of this ability, Rat demonstrates the attributes of industry and prosperity so has a place of honor.

Openwork panel of two long tailed Rats munching grapes, c. 1940 (16" x 7.5"). $200.

Fish is very important in this part of the world as it is a main food source and numerous local occupations are based in it. Fish symbolizes abundance, having more than one needs. Fish has prodigious powers of reproduction so is a symbol of regeneration. Perfectly adapted to its environment, Fish is a symbol of harmony and connubial happiness. In water Fish can move in any direction and this suggests freedom. Fish in water compliments Buddhist doctrine that one who is completely free knows no restraint. Finally, Fish can swim against the current so the attribute of perseverance is also attached. In the world of scholarship, Fish suggests hard work in attaining literary achievement or passing examinations with distinction.

Unusual and intricately carved panel of noble Fish, symbol of abundance and perseverance, with Unicorn, c. 1900 (12.5" x 6"). $350.

Detail of Fish.

An octagonal, lacquer sweets box of red-gold hue with a cover painting of two men and a large fish, c. 1940 (W 8.5", H 3"). $200.

Chapter 5
Plants and Flora

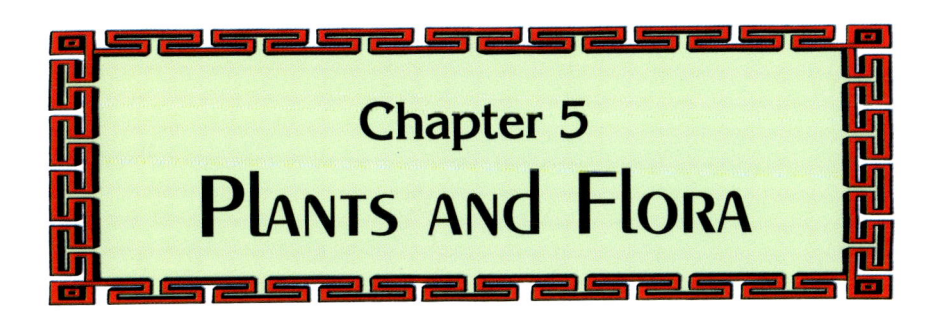

The rendering of vegetation is generally stylized, the product of the imagination of the artist who created it. For this reason, it is difficult to determine the specific plant though artists frequently portray pine and bamboo realistically. While plants have specific meaning, they often overlap and all are meant to convey a good wish.

Pine is always green and is a symbol of longevity. Because it does not wither in winter, pine is a sign for strong friendship that endures through good times and bad. Similarly, bamboo suggests immortality and longevity because it is very durable, evergreen, and flourishes throughout the winter.

Groups of four flowers are intended as the Flowers of the Four Seasons. These are peony for spring, lotus for summer, chrysanthemum for autumn, and prunus (evergreen plants) for winter. Peony is a symbol of the beauty of women, love, and affection. Chrysanthemum represents happiness, joy, and a life of ease, particularly in retirement from public office. Lotus is held in very high esteem and is a symbol for purity because it springs from mud and remains beautiful. Images of Buddha are often seated upon lotus and Buddhist monks seat themselves in the so-called "lotus position." Finally, prunus is a sign of longevity. It also suggests independence and good looks because it blooms at a time when little else grows. Vegetation almost always enters into arts and handicrafts and in whatever form, stylized or not, plants and vegetation are intended to convey happiness and a state of peacefulness.

A lacquer pot of red-gold hue filled with carved lotus flowers, c. 1920 (D 7.5", H 4"). $300.

A carved panel of fruit and flowers, c. 1940 (8.5" x 9.5"). $150.

Lacquer hall entrance decor with floral motifs, suspended from the ceiling to repel evil spirits, c. 1900 (L 15"). $350/pair.

A panel of a vase containing one of the Flowers of The Four Seasons, c. 1900 (12" x 5"). $150.

A sweets dish in the form of a leaf and with carving of grapes at the center, c. 1940 (14.5" x 12"). $250.

A chop sticks holder with pots of flowers carved in relief, c. 1900 (7.5" x 3" x 15"). $350.

Wooden trunk with appliqué flowers and a butterfly at the brass lock, all encased in an interlocking line design, c. 1940 (24" x 14" x 14"). $450.

Paper painting of two noblemen in a garden with attendants who prepare tea, encased in a round metal frame, c. 1920 (D 9.8"). $350.

A porcelain lady's powder box with peony flowers painted on the lid, c. 1900 (D 3.5", H 1.8). $300.

Plants and birds fashioned from metal and in an octagonal frame, c. 1940 (W 14"). $150.

A bronze altar vessel with etched floral decorations and the rim in the form of lotus petals, c. 1920 (H 5.2"). $200.

A silk seat cover with embroidered flower vases and flower stands, symbols of joy in old age, c. 1920 (54" x 25"). $350.

Chapter 6
Objects

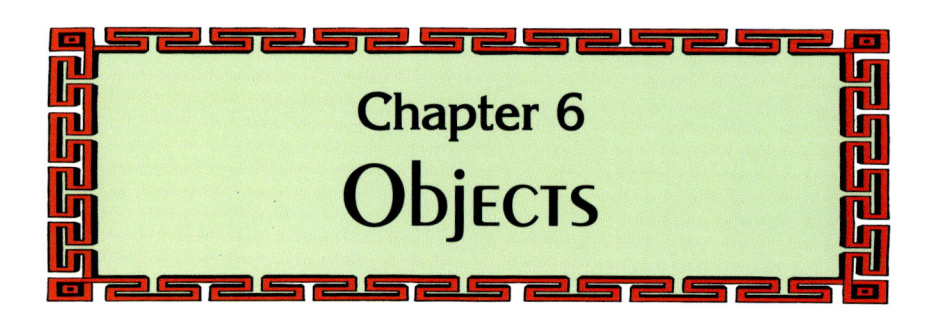

Banner for the pagoda with Animals of Supernatural Power and special objects carved in relief, c. 1940 (28" x 91"). $1200.

A number of particular objects occur in art and are also an integral part of the symbol language. Prominent among these are The Cash, The Lute, The Enflamed Globe, The Scroll, The Fan, The Sacred Text, and The Perfume Bottle.

The Cash is represented by the image of a coin, a symbol of prosperity. The Cash as a circle enclosing a square has implications for officials, suggesting their ability to manage affairs in a smooth fashion with no rough edges to annoy those with whom they come into contact.

The Lute is a musical instrument with, in general, seven strings. Its harmonies echo the harmony of married life and friendship between male and female. It suggests the sublimation of lust to insure marital bliss. For officials, it means purity and moderation. It is also one of the signs of a scholar.

Detail of Unicorn and The Cash.

Detail of The Lute.

The Enflamed Globe is most commonly seen and is usually presented as an object of competition between two Dragons. There are a number of interpretations of the nature of The Enflamed Globe. It is commonly referred to as the moon, but it is also known as a magic jewel, precious pearl, philosopher's stone, or a ruby. When Dragon is present and the object is interpreted as the moon, it is said that Dragon pays homage to the moon. All of these items are precious and sources of wealth and knowledge.

The relationship to the pearl is of particular interest. This interpretation is based in ancient Chinese legends. These stories tell us that pearls are formed in concert with the moon through a secret universal principle. There is one story about a Minister of State with the name Chi Liang who was abroad on service to the throne. On a walk he happened upon a wounded snake and gave it medicine and saved the serpent's life. On a later occasion when he was again abroad, he saw the same snake holding a brilliant pearl in its mouth. The snake informed the Minister that he was the son of His Majesty the Dragon and that the pearl was a gift for the Minister's good deed. The Minister accepted the gift and later presented it to his King.

Detail of The Enflamed Globe.

The Scroll recalls that sacred Buddhist texts are in the form of scrolls. Scrolls are, therefore, symbols of truth. They are also a sign of scholarship.

The Fan reminds us that in ancient times fans were carried on the sleeve or waistband. A fan was used for its intended purpose as well as for punctuating points in conversation. A fan was a luxury and it was unwise to be seen with one at an inappropriate time of the year as this would seem strange and a little ridiculous. But as it was a luxury, fans came to suggest prosperity.

Detail of The Scroll.

Detail of The Fan.

69

The Sacred Text appears on the back of Tortoise and with other creatures and it stands for scholastic achievement and the pursuit of knowledge. It is a common decorative motif, often presented as a set and bound together by a ribbon.

The Perfume Bottle is of importance because it is used for burning incense in special ceremonies and rites, among these, paying homage to the ancestors.

Detail of The Sacred Text on the back of Tortoise who exhales a stream of magic smoke or water from its mouth.

Detail of The Perfume Bottle.

Chapter 7
Tea

Tea, grown mainly in the Central Highlands, is a part of daily life in Vietnam. There are two varieties, green tea for local use and black tea for export. Types range from the ordinary to fragrant teas flavored with the scent of flowers such as chrysanthemum, lotus, and jasmine. Its consumption has become a tradition of the Vietnamese people and over time, the preparation, serving, and drinking of tea has developed a particular social importance in Vietnam. An offer of tea is a gesture of hospitality. But tea is also a drink taken prior to business meetings, scholarly pursuits, and meeting new people. It is served before and after weddings, at funerals, and for farewells. If you have the pleasure to enter a Vietnamese home, chances are you will be offered tea. To be socially correct, you should drink at least a little.

Tea crosses social classes, as common to the humble fisherman on his boat as to trendy urban youth wearing the latest fashions. Of course, economic status determines the type of tea consumed and the paraphernalia surrounding it. Whereas a farmer might have his tea in a banana leaf rolled to form a bowl, the well heeled might drink scented tea from a tea service made with gold and silver. Whatever the means, it is consumed and appreciated across economic classes.

The Nguyen Dynasty (1802-1945) with its new capital at Hue was the catalyst which elevated the status of tea drinking. Members of that royal household used pots and cups with weighted, rounded bottoms that caused slight rocking if disturbed. The effect was intended to symbolize the ability of Vietnam to survive and overcome adversity. The royals loved their tea, even selecting the variety according to the season and devoting attention to details of decor.

In particular, Emperor Tu Duc, who reined from 1848 until 1883, was renowned for drinking lotus-flavored tea. In the afternoon of the day prior to his morning tea his servants rowed in the royal lake and put tea into lotus flowers in blossom. Then they bound up the petals and the tea dried overnight and absorbed the scent of the petals. The following morning, the servants collected the tea from the lotus lake and prepared it for the King for his morning refreshment. The nation followed suit, giving rise to more elaborate ceremonies or, at the very least, more attention to tea and the environment in which it was consumed.

Tea continues to be a vital part of Vietnamese daily life. Along the streets there are places where low tables rest next to a door or under the shade of a tree. The tables have several glass pots with different candies, roasted groundnuts, and sugarcoated cakes resting next to a modest tea container and a tray of cups. Several wooden stools are arranged around the table. This is a makeshift teashop and is a very popular part of Vietnamese street life.

Recently another kind of teashop has appeared in large urban areas. In English, the name translates to

An unusual pair of white and oval-shaped porcelain teacups, c. 1900 (H 1.5"). $250/pair.

"red tea shops" and they offer an interesting mixture of tea, a kind of tea cocktail. The ingredients include flower petals, sugar, honey, milk, and grated ice. Tea is mixed into the blend until a foam appears. Now ready, it goes into a cup. Shops take this further by including other ingredients such as peppermint, lemon, and lotus to add an even more unique character.

Meals in restaurants are followed with complimentary servings of tea, albeit a humble variety. In sum, tea has been around for a long time and will continue to have a very important role in the life of the Vietnamese people and nation.

A porcelain teacup and saucer with painted, stylized floral designs, c. 1950 (D 3.5", H 2.5"). $150.

A porcelain teacup, this side decorated with village scenes, c. 1900 (D 3", H 2.5"). $150.

Poem script of teacup which reflects on the sweet solitude of village life.

Tea saucer with painting of a village scene along with poem script advising that a song needs the right voice, c. 1920 (D 5.5"). $150.

A porcelain tea saucer with painting of a gathering of noblemen beneath pine, c. 1940 (D 5"). $150.

A porcelain tea saucer with painting of two friends who converse in a garden, c. 1900 (D 5"). $150.

A porcelain tea saucer with painting of stylized horses, symbols of perseverance, speed, and strength, in a meadow, c. 1900 (D 4"). $150.

A porcelain teacup strainer with painted natural scenery, c. 1920 (D 8.5", H 3.5"). $400.

A rectangular, lacquer tea tray with scenes from a war legend in mother of pearl inlay, c. 1940 (12" x 7" x 4.5"). $350.

Rectangular, red and gold lacquer tea tray decorated with circular designs carved in openwork, c. 1900 (14" x 8.5" x 5"). $450.

View of the interior.

Detail from a lacquer tea tray with mother of pearl inlay scene of the Eight Immortals upon fabulous creatures that live in or near the sea.

Chapter 8
Habits

Betel

Another custom with very ancient roots is the use of the betel leaf, both for its taste and the euphoric effect it has on the user. In older times betel was integral to the household and it was offered and consumed as a daily social activity. Today it is a dying habit as the cigarette has become more prominent and the pace of life does not permit the more leisurely atmosphere needed for betel consumption.

It is said that betel became popular during the legendary Hong Bang Dynasty under the Hung Vuong Kings. Of course, the Vietnamese love of tales provides an account for betel. There is a story about two brothers, Tan and Lang, who lost their parents when they were very young and developed a strong relationship in their mutual suffering. Schoolmaster Luu, who had a daughter, decided he would raise these boys. When the boys came of age, Schoolmaster Luu chose the brother Tan to marry his daughter. Lang was happy for his brother but suffered in silence because now his older brother had less time for him. One day Lang came back to a darkened house and Tan's wife, in the darkness, mistook him for her husband and greeted him in a very warm manner. Tan arrived at that very instant and became unjustly suspicious and jealous. From that time the brothers became estranged and Lang left the house. He walked long and far into the woods, became tired, and sat beside a river where he began to cry. That night he changed into a rock. Worried and sorrowful, Tan set off to look for his brother. He came to the rock statue where he too fell tired. Leaning against the rock, he wept. The next morning he died embracing the rock. He was transformed to an areca tree. Now the wife went out in search of her husband. She came to the rock and, shedding bitter tears, embraced the trunk of the areca tree. She was changed into a climbing betel plant. The villagers found this area and built a temple in memory of the three to honor conjugal fidelity and brotherly affection. Drought came and devastated the country and the villagers noticed that only this tree and betel plant survived. The King was informed so he went to this spot and chewed the betel leaves and areca nut. He found the taste pleasant and noted the red appearance when mixed in the mouth. And the rest is history.

In reality, the habit is not really one of eating or chewing but is better characterized as sucking. A quid is placed in the side of the mouth and, at times, squeezed between the teeth. There are three main elements, the leaf, the lime, and the nut. Although the term "betel" is used, the nut is from the areca palm, not the betel vine. The leaf of the betel is used to wrap the nut and condiments into packets for consumption. Lime powder is made by burning limestone and then grinding it. To this, water is added. The powder is smeared onto the betel leaf and wrapped in the leaf along with the nut, then consumed.

Betel is enjoyed for its taste and effect. The areca leaf is sweet, the betel bark is hot, and the lime is pungent. Old health books claim that the advantages of betel chewing are a fragrant mouth, improved temperament, and good digestion. Betel gives a mild and relaxing feeling of euphoria. It also reduces appetite, increases salivation and thirst, and turns the saliva a bright red. The

A ceramic lime pot for use in the betel-chewing regime, c. 1920 (D 3.5", H 6.8"). $150.

euphoric feeling accounted for betel's popularity and it soon became associated with hospitality and goodwill.

Betel became a traditional offering at weddings as a symbol of union to death. Sharing betel with an old friend is an expression of gratitude for the friendship. Betel is also present for ceremonies at the altar to the ancestors.

Unlike tea, in these modern times the use of betel is a custom in decline, popular only in some villages and usually among the old. However, we can still find the vestiges of this old custom as wood, porcelain, and bronze containers, simple and elaborate, which people once used to store the betel nut, leaves, and lime powder.

A porcelain lime pot with painted scenes of village life, for use in the betel-chewing regime, c. 1920 (D 3", H 3"). $250.

A lime pot fashioned from the remains of a Cham, gold-plated lime pot at top and a bronze Vietnamese lime pot at bottom, c. 1900 (H 5"). $150.

A square, lacquer tray for betel leaves with scenes from a war legend in mother of pearl inlay, c. 1920 (10" x 10" x 3"). $450.

Detail of the war scene.

Tobacco

It is not known when tobacco became popular in Vietnam, but by the eighteenth century, when Europeans arrived, the Vietnamese were already in the habit of using water pipes. They also used cured, chopped, and powdered tobacco. Craftsmen made containers of various types to store tobacco.

A rectangular tobacco box with mother of pearl inlay butterflies and flowers, c. 1920 (6.5" x 3.5" x 3.5"). $300.

A porcelain water pipe with a scene of five companions at a game table, c. 1940 (D 5", H 8). $350.

A porcelain water pipe in the form of a slipper and with painted flowers, c. 1940 (L 6", H 7.5"). $350.

An unusual round and green shell tobacco box with serpent Dragons who encircle Goat, a symbol of male potency, on the lid, c. 1940 (D 5.5", H 1.5"). $250.

83

Chapter 9
Scholars

Scholars have historically enjoyed a revered status in Vietnam. Aspects of the world of the scholars and scholarship are reflected in several of these pieces as implements, documents, and items adorned with characters and script.

The special status of the scholar is deeply rooted in the competition for careers in the Mandarinate, or civil service, in Vietnam's history. The Confucian system of education represented by this examination replaced an earlier system under which the Buddhist clergy were the source of education. While under Chinese domination, Vietnam absorbed much of the Chinese educational system. These examinations began as early as 1045 in Hue and successful candidates became Mandarins. The examinations were extremely competitive and few passed. Between 1075 and 1918, when the last Mandarinate Examinations were held, only 2000 candidates passed the doctoral degree.

The Mandarinate Examinations determined who would serve the state, using knowledge of education and culture as a basis. The emphasis was not on technical or administrative skills, but on academic knowledge of literary works, Chinese rhetoric, and ancient poetry. Future servants of the state were expected to have a perfect grounding and knowledge of classical culture. This tended to solidify the ruling class on the basis of a common mentality and undoubtedly served as one means for the Chinese to maintain their influence. Successful candidates went on to serve the state and were inclined to uphold the purity of state doctrines. This was one of the key elements on the road to involvement in the machinery of power and those who passed were regarded as scholars and revered. They ran all levels of administration in Vietnam.

Technically, any male, regardless of his background, could study and take the competitive examinations and, if successful, become a Mandarin. In practice the process was not quite this open, as it required numerous references from local officials. This produced a climate ripe for interference and preference in the process. In addition, the authorities deemed certain people unworthy and they were excluded. Among the excluded were menial workers, actors, and criminals. As well, three generations of their progeny were also prohibited from taking the examinations.

There were two branches of the Mandarinate, civil (or literary), and military. Traditionally, Mandarins in the literary branch were afforded more prestige than those in the military branch. The literary examinations gave more importance to intellectual qualities while the military examinations assessed physical aptitude. In the literary field there were four examinations to be taken to reach the top of the Mandarinate. These were the provincial examinations, regional examinations, national competitive examinations, and the court examination.

At the first stage, the provincial level, students had to pass four lower level literary tests administered by state employed professors. This phase required excellent ability in the fields of interpretation, verse, composition, and philosophy in order to pass. At the appointed time thousands of students took this examination in open-air camps set up for this purpose and guarded by the army to prevent any outside help for students. There were four test sessions, each lasting twenty-four hours and given at three to four day intervals. Each test started at 3 a.m. when the student was given special paper and sent back to his tent where he wrote his responses until the following midnight.

Success at the provincial level was necessary to proceed to the regional stage. In addition, candidates had to secure numerous character references to proceed. This pre-screening successfully accomplished, they could then be admitted as a candidate for the four regional examinations. The regional examinations were much harder and students passing three of the tests received the title of "bachelor" while those passing all four were designated "licentiates." All other candidates failed.

Licentiates could proceed to the national competitive examinations for the doctoral degree. The Emperor himself made up the questions for the examination and students who scored highest were eligible to take the court examination. Those students who scored in the second group were eligible to retake the examination. In the meantime, they were registered with the Ministry of Personnel and Interior for future government employment either as a prefect or assistant prefect.

By this time, the numbers had been drastically reduced and the remaining candidates would proceed to the final court examination. The Emperor personally conducted this examination and only the three who scored highest were proclaimed doctors first class. The other candidates were awarded doctor's degrees in lower classes. The elite three were entitled to appointments as provincial judicial officers while the others could secure positions in a ministry or prefecture. All successful candidates returned home with great personal honor and respect and brought honor and pride to their families.

As in the past, students in Vietnam today remain very serious about their education, study hard, are academically competitive, and show great respect, even reverence, for teachers. They are very occupied with examinations, particularly the national examinations for entry into university. And as in the past, high academic achievement brings personal and family honor.

A wooden statue of a civil Mandarin in vestments including gold gilt headdress, c. 1940 (6.8" x 5.5" x 18.5"). $350.

Porcelain figure of a seated scholar, c. 1940 (H 8"). $250.

A painted, stone figure of a proud Mandarin on horseback, c. 1940 (4" x 7.5" x 17.5"). $400.

Case for an official's stamp with openwork carvings of an Animal of Supernatural Power on each side, c. 1930 (8" x 11 x 11"). $550.

An ivory stamp with case, for an official, c. 1900 (L 2.2"). $350

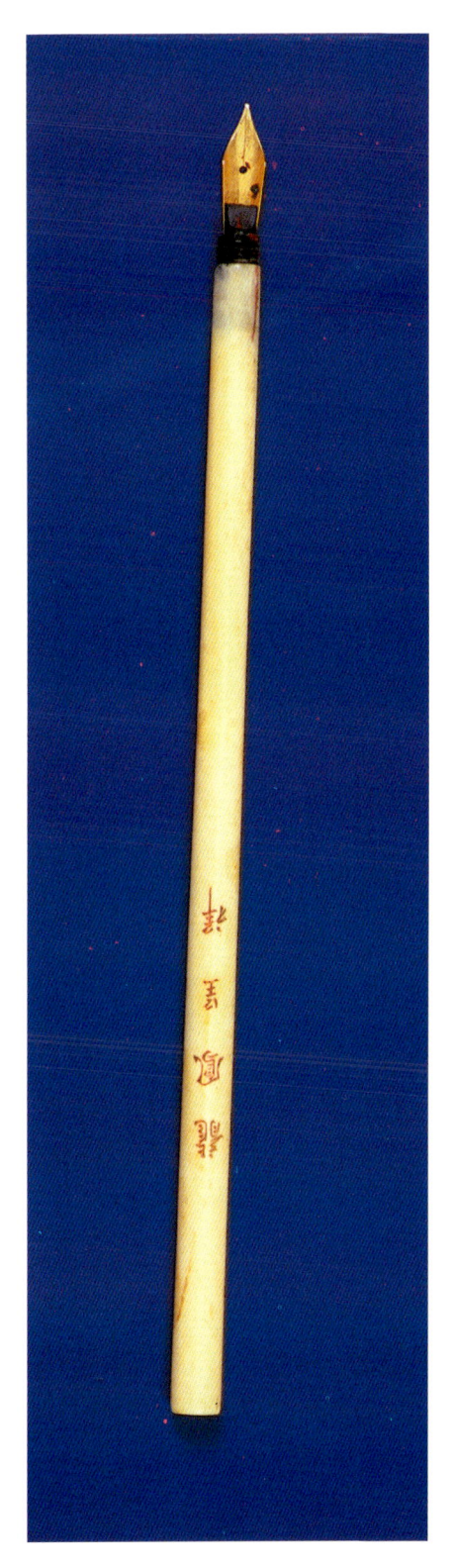

Ivory pen tube with scripted "100 happinesses" wish; original animal hair tip replaced by a gold tip from an old pen, c. 1900 (L 8"). $600.

87

A lacquer brush pot with painted floral designs, c. 1940 (H 6"). $250.

A porcelain ink well with a painted scene of noblemen at leisure under pine, c. 1920 (D 5.2", H 2.5"). $400.

A copper ink well stand with two wells, c. 1900 (L 5.5", H 6"). $350.

A rectangular, lacquer letterbox with slide-out cover and paintings of birds and natural surroundings, c. 1920 (7" x 4.5" x 3"). $250.

A scholar's lacquer writing box with ivory trim and an ink well at the center of the removable tray, c. 1940 (10" x 5.5" x 5.5"). $350.

Student's examination box with five sections in the removable tray, c. 1940 (14" x 8" x 7"). $350.

A table cabinet with roll-up door, for letters and writing implements, c. 1920 (16" x 10" x 17"). $450.

A red and gold lacquer scroll screen sits on a stylized Unicorn base, c. 1920 (18" x 13" x 16"). $550.

Detail from a decree in the time of Emperor Khai Dinh granting permission and an area for a celebration, c. 1920.

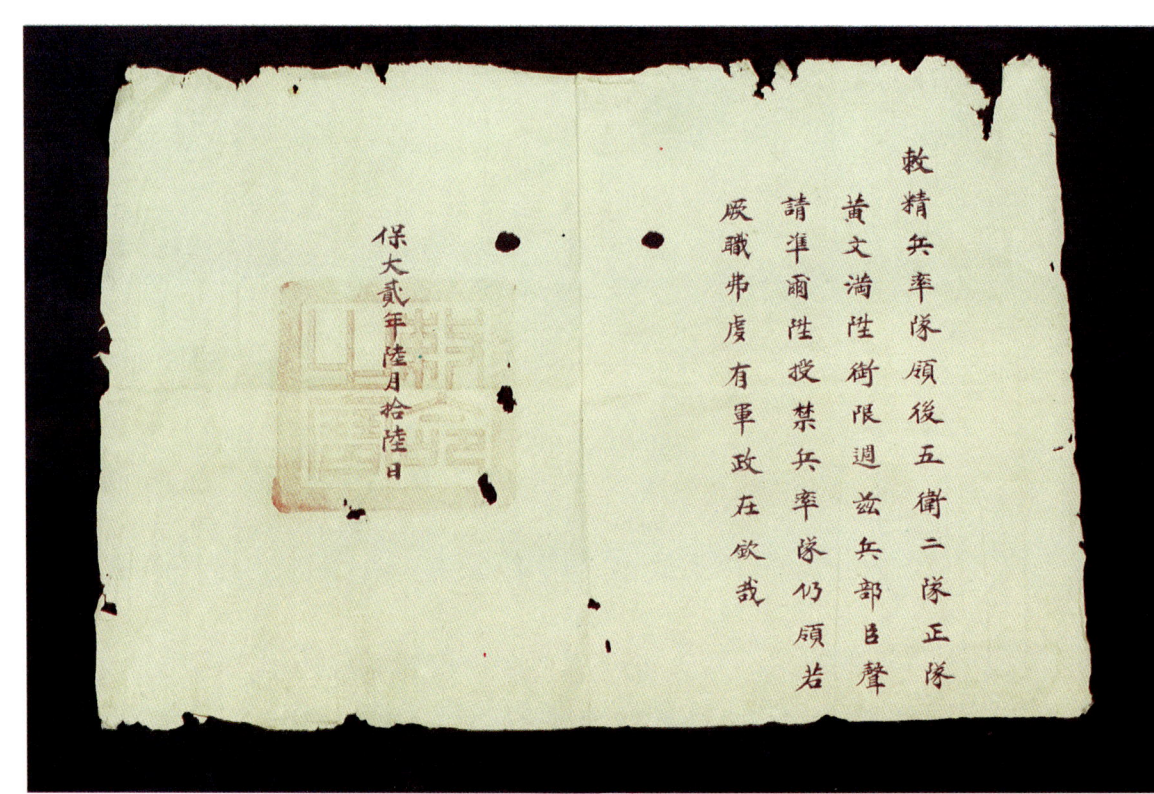

A promotion notice for an official granted in the time of Emperor Bao Dai, c. 1940. $100.

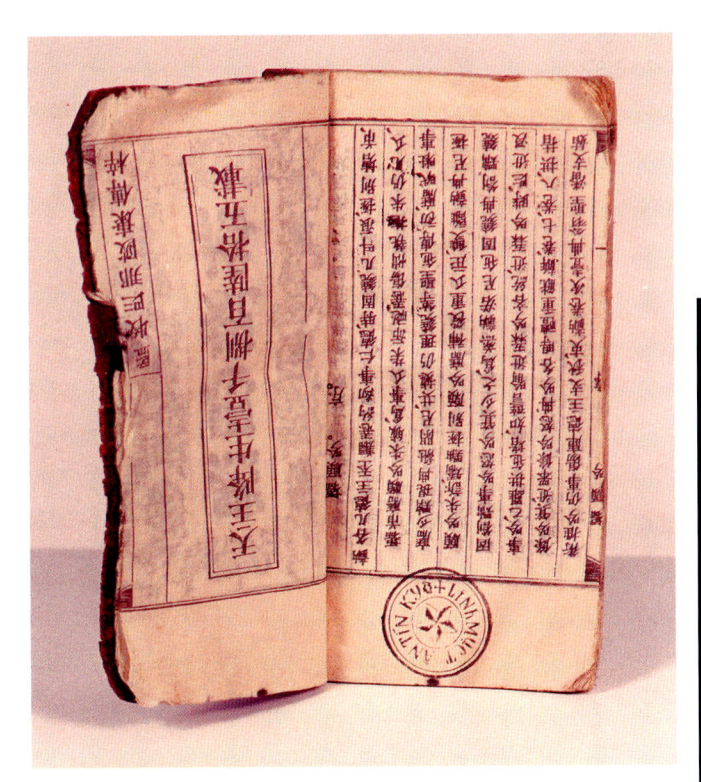

Student text on ethics, written on cloth, c. 1865 (6 x 10). $250.

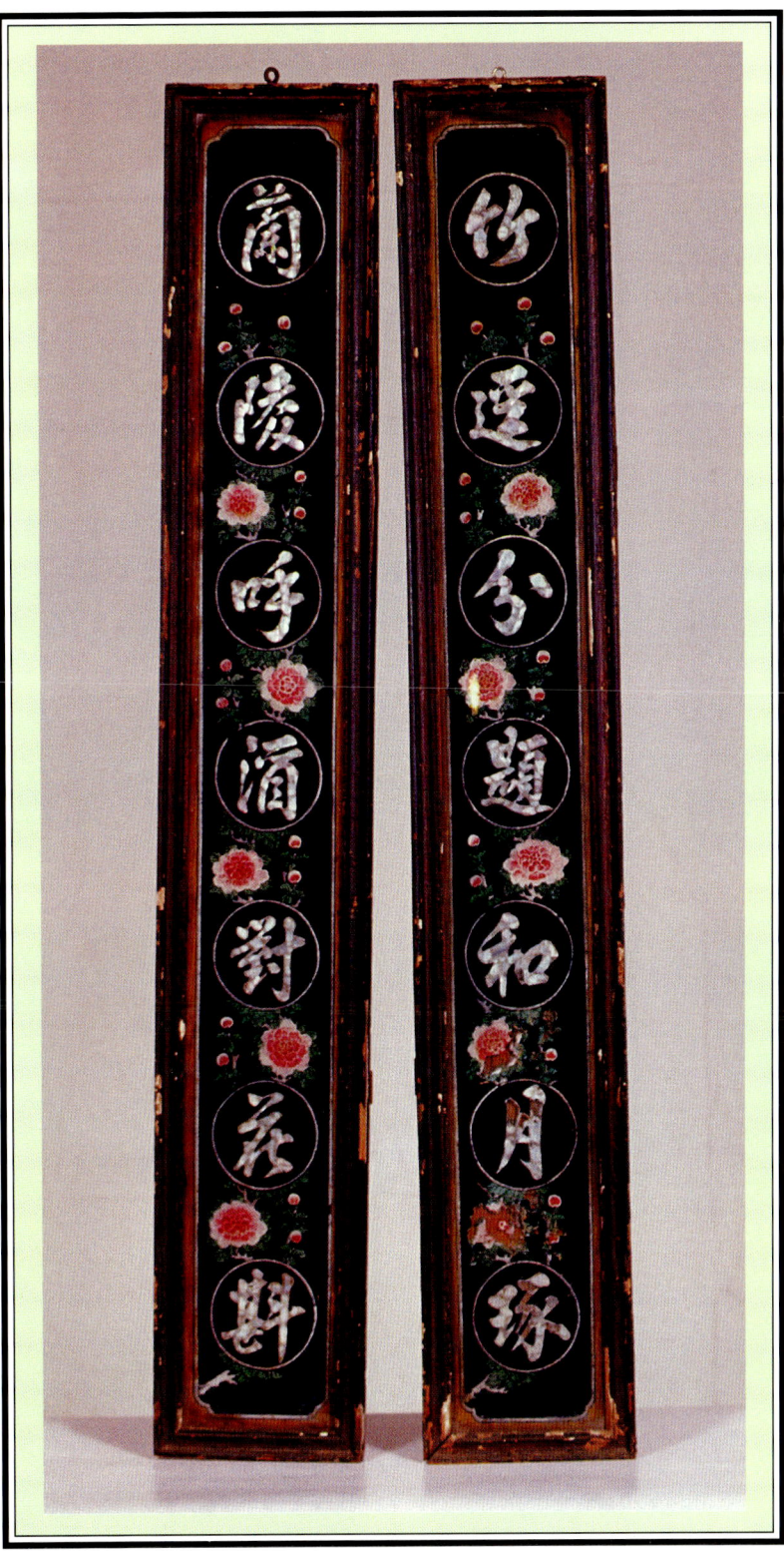

Unusual glass sentence panel with mother of pearl flowers and poem script about finding victory in adversity, c. 1920 (50" x 8"). $700/pair.

93

Sentence panel with bamboo appliqué designs and a poem on the constancy of noble responsibilities, c. 1940 (70" x 8.5"). $350.

Detail of Unicorn.

Gold gilt, ceremonial headdress for a Mandarin, c. 1900 (H 17"). $1100.

Chapter 10
The Chinese

A panel of an Immortal among clouds (11" x 11"), c. 1900. $200.

Vietnam has had a difficult struggle to maintain its national identity and freedom in the face of foreigners who sought to control it. Just look at the street signs in any city and you will find names like Hai Ba Trung, Le Loi, Tran Hung Dao — all patriots who would not accept a Vietnam that was under the control of a foreign power and who fought for that noble cause, an independent Vietnam. These are only a few. There are many, many others who gave their lives to or for this quest.

This collection includes items sourced in Vietnam's relationship with the Chinese, French, and Khmer. All occupied and controlled Vietnam or parts of it at a point in time, holding it as part of an external empire or as a colony. All met resistance and were eventually defeated

A table cosmetics cabinet with appliqué stone carvings of ladies of means, c. 1900 (15.5" x 10" x 11"). $550.

Detail of ladies.

97

and expelled. Two of these groups, the Chinese and Khmer are, respectively, the first and third largest ethnic minorities in Vietnam today. All have had an influence on Vietnam, however, the influence and role of the Chinese by far surpassed that of these or any other outsiders.

There are about 2.3 million ethnic Chinese living in Vietnam, mostly in southern Vietnam, and they are the largest minority group. The Chinese have long been a vital force in the economy of the country in such areas as rice trading, milling, real estate, banking, and mining. That influence stretched beyond economy and into the arts and crafts where in style and content, one finds that Vietnamese arts often reveal heavy Chinese influence.

At the end of the eighteenth century tens of thousands of Chinese immigrants arrived in Vietnam. With them came their arts and crafts. Some settled in Hue but most settled outside of Saigon, now Ho Chi Minh City, and founded Cholon. Cholon today remains a thriving area and still retains a strong Chinese character. It is called "Chinatown." However, this was not the first wave of Chinese immigrants. Long before this time Vietnam was shaped by China, and this mass immigration only solidified and strengthened those influences. Effectively, Vietnam was under Chinese domination during the time 111 BC to 939 AD.

The first period of Chinese occupation ended in 39 AD, the result of an armed revolt led by the Trung Sisters (Trung Trac and Trung Nhi) who are national martyrs, and known as "Hai Ba Trung" (The Two Trung Sisters). But just three years later, the Chinese armies overran them and reaffirmed Chinese rule. Rather than succumb, the Trung Sisters chose suicide and martyrdom, drowning themselves in the Hat Giang River in 43 AD in the second month of the Lunar Year.

The subsequent period of Chinese rule was more brutal in one sense, but included a stronger and more focused ideological element. In addition to repression and force, the Chinese included measures such as moving mass numbers of Chinese into Vietnam as immigrants. This was done with an eye to blending the population and changing the mindset of the people. Chinese rulers also imposed their laws, provided for the teaching of their language, and promoted their way of life.

While Chinese administrators replaced most former local officials and ran things, some members of the Vietnamese aristocracy were allowed to fill lower positions in the bureaucracy. These lower level bureaucrats were well schooled in Chinese cultural, religious, and political traditions. While none of this erased the memory of former traditions, it did render the elite Vietnamese more receptive to Chinese culture. The Vietnamese people continued their struggle to maintain their own identity, but such

Detail of characters on cover identifying the company.

A food box for a company, c. 1900 (8" x 14.5" x 15"). $250.

measures as these had an enormous effect on the national psychology.

The Chinese domination of Vietnam was never without its price, as the Vietnamese continued to resist and there were periodic, violent upheavals. However, the cumulative effect of Chinese dominance was to profoundly, perhaps permanently, mold and shape the life of Vietnam. Along with the Chinese came quite a bit of baggage. Chinese writing, Confucianism, science, medicine, and architecture were areas where the Chinese would exert a strong influence. Buddhism, Taoism, and the civil code of Confucianism also came with the Chinese conquerors.

This influence is clearly seen in modern Vietnamese arts and crafts. Although there are items created with Vietnamese tastes and sensibilities, there are numerous examples of Vietnamese works inspired by a Chinese aesthetic. Also, there are significant numbers of original Chinese pieces. In some instances, these items were created in country for economic and religious reasons, and, in others, they made the journey to Vietnam from China. It is a difficult distinction to make with precision. In either case, these pieces are here to remind us of Vietnam's past and to give us visual pleasure in the present.

Lacquer box for the wedding ceremony with gold paintings from a legend and natural surroundings, c. 1900 (D 10", H 4"). $400.

Detail of painting along the container rim of a bird approaching a branch.

A round, black, and gold lacquer sweets box with a cover painting of a nobleman with his attendant, c. 1900 (D 14", H 4.5"). $400.

Detail of cover painting.

An unusual lacquer sweets tray, cover missing, with three sections above openwork carvings of five noblemen at the pavilion, c. 1900 (8" x 3" x 4"). $350.

Reverse of tray with floral carvings.

Unusual lacquer sweets box with relief scene of the procession for a dignitary on the cover and carvings along the sides, c. 1900 (16" x 8" x 3.5"). $850.

View of tray compartment and serpent Dragons at the base who contend for a precious object.

Rectangular, red lacquer sweets box cover with painting of an Immortal atop a giant toad and an attendant with a banner, c. 1900 (13.5" x 6.5"). $250.

Six-sided lacquer sweets tray cover with a nobleman and attendant in a garden as Crane, for longevity, looks on, c. 1900 (7" x 13"), $250.

Lacquer sweets tray, cover missing, with carving of noblemen flanked by attendants holding vessels, c. 1900 (L 10.5", H 3.8"). $350.

A hexagonal sweets dish with a gilt rim and center painting of an attendant in a garden, c. 1900 (L 11.5", H 1.5"). $250.

A hexagonal sweets dish with painting of an attendant in a garden. $250.

Lacquer sweets tray, cover missing, with flowers flanked by attendants holding vessels, revolving Lions on the base, c. 1900 (L 15", H 10"). $350.

A pair of cloisonné sweets dishes with paintings of noblemen at leisure and with attendants, beneath poem script, c. 1900 (W 4.4"). $250/pair.

A panel depicting a fine featured elder with four like-featured younger men, c. 1900 (7" x 11"). $200.

An unusual panel of two noblemen on a hunt and an attendant wearing deerskin as camouflage and holding a food bucket to attract the prey, c. 1900 (8" x 18"). $400.

Detail of the nobleman hunter, his bow and arrow at the ready.

Panel of a nobleman archer on a galloping horse as his arrow finds its mark, c. 1900 (14" x 6.5"). $200.

Detail of a lacquer panel of a nobleman in a garden with two attendants.

Lacquer panel of several noblemen at various activities and with attendants, and with designs carved at the back, c. 1900 (11" x 18"). $400.

Detail of the interlocking line carving at back of panel and the Buddhist swastika at the right, symbol for endless longevity and "Heart of Buddha."

Lacquer panel of two noblemen who converse at the pavilion, c. 1900 (6" x 3" x 11"). $450.

Gold lacquer panel of noblemen conversing inside the pavilion, c. 1900 (10.5" x 13"). $450.

110

A lacquer panel depicting a scene at a tribunal, c. 1900 (8" x 12"). $450.

Window panel with carvings of Immortals, attendants, and a central holy man, c. 1900 (30" x 21.5"). $750.

111

Detail of holy man, attendants.

Detail of an Immortal, attendants.

Detail of the couple.

A window screen panel with central carving of a older and happily married couple, c. 1920 (32.5" x 11.5"). $300.

Crabs and The Perfume Bottle carved in openwork, c. 1900 (6.5 x 22 in). $350.

113

Lacquer bed headboard with five circular panels painted with scenes of noblemen and attendants in natural surroundings, c. 1900 (17" x 72"). $550.

Detail of a nobleman with his attendant.

Detail of a nobleman with his attendant.

114

An unusual, horn-shaped, red and gold lacquer gunpowder case topped by two Lions standing watch over warriors in battle, c. 1900 (6.2" x 7"). $1100.

Porcelain screen in a wood frame with painting of a nobleman taking leave from his wife and script on the depth of marital love, c. 1940 (20" x 7" x 18.5"). $300.

A glass painting of a pensive, seated lady having tea and holding a fan, c. 1900 (18.5" x 14"). $450.

A cinnabar box for powdered tobacco with a carved scene of a man at harvest, c. 1900 (H 2.8"). $450.

Reverse with carving of a man walking leisurely and holding a fan.

Chapter 11
The Khmer

The Khmer in Vietnam are the descendents of a great civilization whose armies once conquered and controlled southern Vietnam as well as other parts of Southeast Asia. The Khmer Empire, synonymous with the splendor and majesty of Ankor Wat, was a formidable force from the ninth to the thirteenth centuries when it was at its peak.

The Khmers controlled what today are Laos, Thailand, Cambodia, and southern Vietnam. However, domestic instability in the thirteenth to fourteenth centuries played into the hands of the Vietnamese and Thai, who managed to put their squabbles aside and combine forces against a common enemy. Gradually they weakened the grip of the Khmers, leading to the end of the rule of the Khmer in Vietnam and their confinement to the area we know today as Cambodia.

Now, the Khmer live along the southwestern border of Vietnam from Tay Ninh Province to Can Tho Province, and along the Mekong River. Their language is called "Khmer." Presently, there are about one million Khmer Krom (Cambodians) living in Vietnam and they are the third largest minority group. An agricultural people, the Khmer have a long tradition in wet rice cultivation and animal husbandry. They live in villages or hamlets and in thatch roof, bamboo houses that rest on stilts. Each village and hamlet has a chief who acts as the liaison between the people and the central government. Beyond that, there is no political structure. In turn, local leadership is divided into two parts. The chief is the authority in secular matters while the head Buddhist monk oversees religious issues.

The pagoda is the center of Khmer cultural activity and the Khmer have built more than 400 pagodas in the south of Vietnam. It is here where monks pass on traditions to young people who improve their knowledge and learn the Khmer system of writing. It is here where the yearly traditional festivals, ceremonies, and rituals, such as the celebration of the birth of Buddha and the special rite of asking forgiveness of the crimes of the dead, are held.

Though they maintain their own language and beliefs, the Khmer are well absorbed into the Vietnamese community and the relationship is one of relative harmony. Many Khmer have acquired the language and culture of the ethnic Vietnamese. As well, they often share the same religion and customs and there has been significant intermarriage between these groups.

There are many Khmer arts and crafts available in and around Ho Chi Minh City. Khmer arts are easily distinguished because of unique differences in colors and style. As with the crafts of the Vietnamese, much of this work is driven by religious beliefs but there are also items of a secular nature.

Gilt figure of a temple guardian, c. 1920 (2.5" x 3" x 5.5"). $350.

Ivory figure of a female, Khmer deity, c. 1920 (H 3"). $550.

A pair of gold lacquer Buddhas seated upon thrones, c. 1950 (H 7"). $250/pair.

Detail, the water offering of Elephant is accepted.

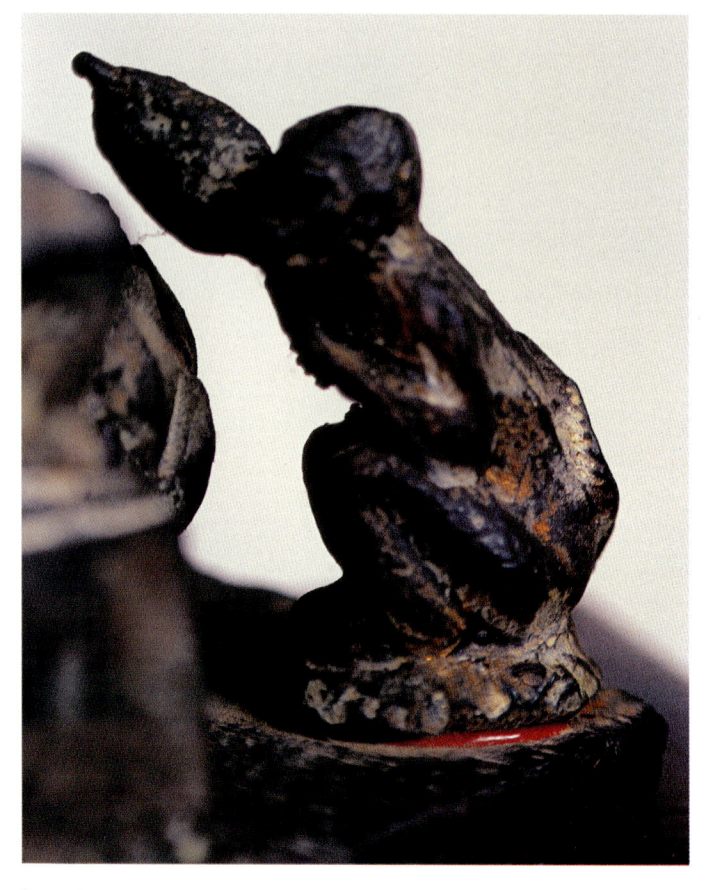

Wood statue of Buddha on his throne recalling the legend of the offerings of Elephant and Monkey, c. 1920 (H 9.5). $550.

Detail, the honey offering of Monkey is refused for it comes from a living creature.

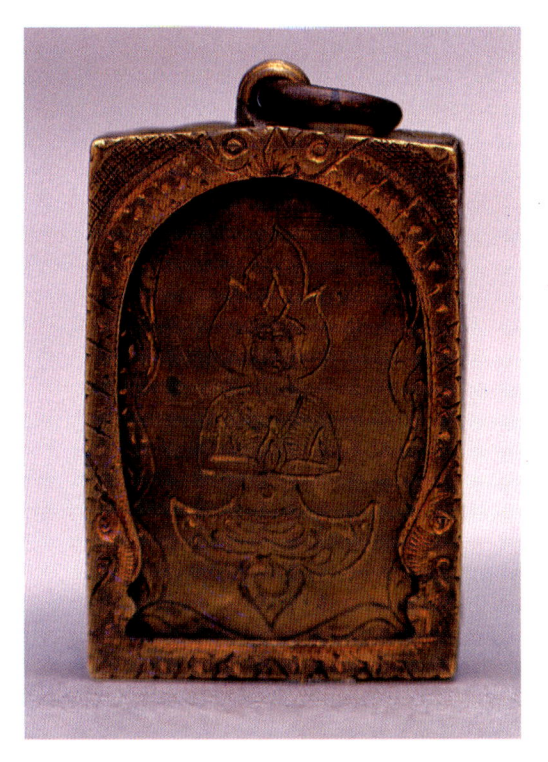

A gold-plated protective amulet with an etching of a Buddhist angel, c. 1900 (H 1"). $200.

A portrait frame for the altar, painted with floral designs at the top and bottom, c. 1950 (9.5 x 9" x 23.5"). $200.

A painting on silk cloth depicting Lord Buddha with attendant angels, c. 1920 (36" x 24"). $450.

A pair of round altar containers for vessels of holy water, c. 1920 (D 5.5", H 12.5"). $400/pair.

A wooden altar stand for incense, offerings, and religious ornaments, c. 1900 (11.5" x 16.5" x 29"). $550.

Detail of serpent Dragon.

123

A wooden altar stand for religious ornaments with a painting on the back panel of Lord Buddha seated in the lotus position, c. 1900 (11" x 16.5" x 31"). $550.

Detail of painting of Lord Buddha.

Gold lacquer ornament which hangs from ceiling to repel evil spirits, suspended by tread strung through carved beads, c. 1940 (L 19"). $350/pair.

Round, red and gold lacquer betel box with a sectioned tray and carved designs of flowers encircling the box, c. 1920 (D 7.5", H 4"). $300.

Hall entrance hanging.

125

A round, lacquer betel box with a sectioned tray and gilt decoration, c. 1920 (D 8", H 5"). $300.

An eight-sided betel tray with mother of pearl decoration, c. 1900 (8.5" x 8.5" x 2.5"). $450.

Below the betel box is a red and black, six-sided betel tray, c. 1920 (4.5" 9" x 9" x 4.5"). $250.

Chapter 12
The French

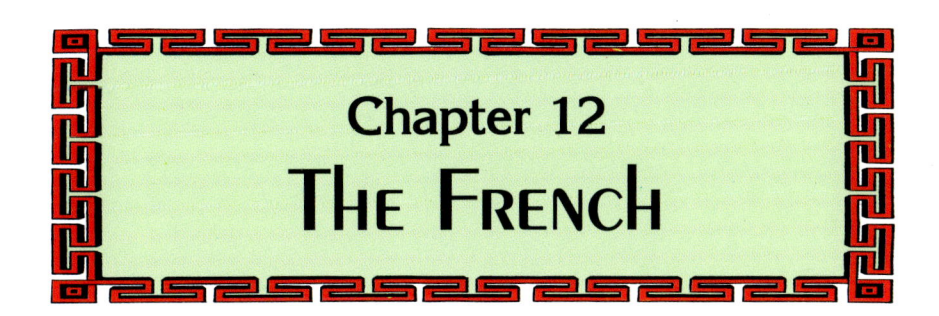

In time, the French came as conquerors and the Vietnamese were no more willing to be controlled by the French than they had been to be ruled by others. The French established tentative rule over areas in the south in the mid-19th century and called the area "Cochin China." They were met with forceful resistance but ultimately, through superior armaments, the French subdued the land, though not the will of the people to resist. By the turn of the century, the French had established control over resources like alcohol, salt, and opium. Politically, French nationals administered the country.

The French Foreign Ministry reported 450,000 Christian converts in Vietnam in 1841. The Vietnamese Christians were, for the most part, organized into villages and included all social levels from workers of the land to landowners. The Christian villages had their distinct customs, schools, and hierarchy, leaving less reverence for Confucianism. For the French, conversion represented one means to win the hearts and minds of the people.

At the end of World War II, Vietnamese leaders held the hope of gaining their independence from France. During the war, Vietnam was under the control of the Japanese, though the Japanese authorities had allowed the existence of a French puppet administration. The Vietnamese had actively assisted the Allied Forces, hoping that this would lead to national independence. Those hopes crashed when, after the defeat of the Japanese, France retained control of Vietnam. Resistance to the French continued and war broke out in 1946. This bitter and bloody conflict would last for eight long and difficult years.

The French formed a Vietnamese government under Bao Dai, Vietnam's last Emperor who had abdicated in 1945, in the effort to lend legitimacy to their cause. However, in 1954 the French were overrun and decisively defeated at Dien Bien Phu and forced to the negotiation table at Geneva. Bao Dai would eventually go in exile to France where he died in 1997.

The Geneva negotiations provided for the division of the country along the 17th parallel. Control of the North was ceded to the Viet Minh forces led by Ho Chi Minh and control of the South was given to the French and their Vietnamese supporters. To avoid permanent separation, a political protocol called for national elections to reunify the country two years after the signing of the Geneva treaty.

In Vietnam, there is much to be found to remind us of its past relationship with France. Among these are pieces which may have come from France with French nationals. Others may have once been the property of wealthy Vietnamese who visited France and returned with items they purchased. In other cases they are items produced in Vietnam for export.

A silk fan with a hand-painted young gentleman and lady, c. 1950 (9" x 17"). $200.

Wine glasses with metal coasters, produced for export, c. 1940 (H 2.5"). $50 per glass/coaster.

Colored wine glasses produced for export, c. 1940 (D 1.8", H 3.2"). $25 per glass.

A glass ink well with three wells which have silver-plated covers and a pen compartment, c. 1950 (10" x 3.5" x 3"). $200.

A glass ink well with a single well and a silver-plated cover, c. 1950 (5" x 5" x 3"). $150.

129

Porcelain stand for a teakettle with painting of a young woman and a cat, encircled by flowers, for export, c. 1920 (D 8"). $350/pair.

Porcelain teakettle stand with painted scene of a young woman, a child, and a dog.

Porcelain saucers for export decorated with flowers and pavilions, c. 1945 (D 7.2"). $100 per piece.

Chapter 13
Beliefs

ANCESTOR WORSHIP

First and foremost, religious belief in Vietnam is rooted in ancient notions of a world alive with gods and spirits and the need for guidance and protection. Deities, benevolent and malicious, are in stones, the mountains, the trees, the streams, the rivers, and the air itself. Not only are they present, but they must also be appeased through rituals.

Spirits abound from womb to tomb. At birth, souls of higher and lower rank take over the body and leave it at death in search of another existence. Though departed from this earth, the dead are very much a part of the life of the world of the living. This is expressed as Ancestor Worship or the Cult of the Ancestors. It is the Vietnamese take on a precept common to many religions, life does not end with death.

Ancestor Worship is a consuming belief that reveals Confucian influences that stressed obedience to authority. Simply put, this means the dead must be honored on a par with the living and it places deceased relatives at the very heart of the household. The explicit expression of this belief can be seen in most homes in the form of an altar to the deceased ancestors. If you see such an altar, you will have seen the essence of religion and belief in Vietnam, worship of the ancestors. Candles, incense, small stands, and portrait frames with images of the deceased are among the items to be found here. Perhaps there will be a wooden tablet with words inscribed in gold lacquer in honor of the deceased. In this area of the home, discord should dissolve and families should come together. It is here before the family altar that the dead are honored, marriages are consecrated, and matters of family importance are discussed.

Respect for the dead mandates set dates for special ceremonies to honor and remember the deceased. Day 50 and day 100 after the death are times for memorial rites at the family altar. These rites are also held during other ceremonies and on the birthday of the deceased. On the last day of the lunar year, there is a ceremony to invite the ancestors home to celebrate Lunar New Year. Responsibility to the ancestors is the core and at the deepest root of Vietnamese beliefs and religious expression.

The living appeal to spirits in behalf of dead relatives to make their journey into the world beyond easier. For themselves, the living plead for a better life in this world. Family members may seek help in business or examinations. They might request the birth of a child or relief from illness. The rites and ceremonies involve incense, offerings, even burning a special kind of paper representing an offering of gold.

If the deceased led a meritorious life, the survivors can benefit, but if not, the survivors might suffer the consequences. In either case, contact with the deceased continues to insure their peace and the security of those left in this world. Death may open the door to another world, but the dead remain very close to the living. The central message is that the dead are always with us, can never be ignored, and must always be honored.

At the village level, departed locals who exhibited special achievements or qualities in life may, in death, be deemed to have special protective powers. If so, they may be deified and worshipped. This group has included military leaders, scholars, royalty, and others. Consequently, Vietnam remains fertile ground for fortune-tellers, seers, astrologers, horoscope casters, I-Ching diviners, or palm readers who can open a window to the supernatural world and seek guidance from benevolent spirits. With the assistance of mediums, the living seek advice in determining the best time for matters ranging from taking on new projects or responsibilities to how space should be utilized in a new house.

These beliefs in the spirit world are commonly held, whatever age or level of education, and they have found their way into all other forms of religious expression. They account for the presence of small shrines inside or near the entry of houses and shops where incense burns and offerings of food, usually fruit, wither away, ostensibly consumed by the passing spirits. They explain the presence of mirrors bordered with special geometric designs that rest at the entrance of homes and businesses to prevent the entry of harmful spirits, or the image of Sacred Tiger strategically placed to chase evil spirits away.

Blending with and adding to these ancient beliefs are the three great religions of East Asia, Buddhism, Taoism, and Confucianism. All of these beliefs came to Vietnam during the period of Chinese control. The Vietnamese people have been molded by these belief systems and they have become a fundamental part of national life.

A lacquer offering stand for a perfume bottle, flowers, or other ritual items, c. 1920 (27" x 5.5" x 8"). $350.

Altar slide-out frame, now a mirror, for a portrait of an ancestor, c. 1940 (W 15", H 27"). $250.

An altar slide-out frame with carved floral designs, for a portrait of an ancestor, c. 1940 (W 11.5", H 16"). $250.

Wine vessels for the ancestral altar, red lacquer over bronze, c. 1940 (H 4.5"). $300/pair.

A wood figure of a seated, fierce looking, benevolent protector, c. 1900 (H 9"). $250.

A banner in honor of an ancestor, c. 1950 (57.5" x 23.5"). $450.

A painted wood figure of a seated, peaceful looking, benevolent protector, c. 1900 (H 6"). $300.

Buddhism

Buddhism came to Vietnam in the second and third centuries from China and India. It is the religion of first importance in Vietnam teaching that humankind is originally pure. Contemplation can lead back to that original purity. Progression towards perfection is in stages. At the first stage is attention; the mind focuses on one thought. The second stage is the state of joy, raising the level of intuition. The third stage is happiness that ushers in perfect calm. Finally, the fourth stage is indifference. It is at this stage when one begins the journey towards absolute goodness. Central to Vietnamese Buddhism is the belief in bodhisattvas, holy beings who have already achieved salvation but chose to remain in the world to help relieve the suffering of mankind rather than enter nirvana, or the state of perfect happiness.

There have been significant offshoots from Buddhism, namely the Buu Son Ky Huong and Hoa Hao Movements. The former grew in the 1850s from the belief that Buddhism had lost its purpose through mindless repetition of prayers and expensive ceremonies and offerings. It represented a return to values such as hard work and frugality and set rich and poor on equal footing. Rather than a congregational or monastic orientation, it was family-centered. The latter, Hoa Hoa, flourished in the 1940s and, as its main divergence, advocated the injection of religious values into politics. Followers believed religious people should be politically active since religion and politics were both concerned with salvation. Neither strand altered or sought to change the fundamental belief in spirits, the spirit world, or responsibility to ancestors.

Statue of Lord Buddha upon a Dragon throne, flanked by holy attendants, c. 1940 (W 17", H 11"). $450.

A folk carving of the female deity Quan Am, Goddess of Mercy, who saves souls from the torments of hell, c. 1940 (4" x 3.5" x 10"). $300.

An oil painting of a Venerable Buddhist monk in vestments, c. 1950 (24.5" x 18"). $450.

A pair of lacquer goblets, representing sacrifice, for the altar, c. 1940 (D 2.2", H 3.5"). $150/pair.

Red lacquer, oval-shaped, ceremonial case for vessels of holy water, handle in the form of a flower, c. 1940 (H 10"). $300.

A pair of altar candle stands, c. 1940 (H 9.5"). $300/pair.

An altar with carved serpent Dragon motifs rests on a base with curved legs, c. 1900 (19" x 16" x 25.5"). $1800.

Side view of altar.

Detail of serpent Dragon panel.

139

Taoism

Taoist doctrine has been very influential and can claim a large following. As its center, the faith attempts to explain how humankind fits into the universal order. Humans themselves are equated with the universe. The head is the celestial vault, the feet are the earth, the left eye is the moon, and the right eye is the sun. Veins are rivers and the bladder is the ocean. Hairs are the stars and planets. The grinding of teeth represents thunder and so forth. One with knowledge of how to use elements in the material world can do anything at will. Taoism has numerous divinities. Chief among these is the August Emperor of Jade who lives in the center of the sky in an immense palace. Incantations, exorcism, charms, amulets, magic, and sorcery are all essential to Taoism.

Taoism also provides some very popular and accessible deities known as the Eight Taoist Immortals. According to legend, they became eternal through the mastery of nature's secrets. Each has special attributes and areas of responsibility.

Immortal Lam Thai Hoa, who can be a man or woman, is the patron of florists and a symbol for delusive pleasure. A chemist and protector of the sick, Immortal Ly Thiet Quai walks with the help of an iron crutch and carries the Elixir of Immortality and other magical medicines and potions in his double gourd. Immortal Ha Tien Co is a woman who assists with household affairs and always carries a lotus flower. Somewhat more popular in the public imagination is Immortal Han Tuong Tu who plays his magic flute, is the patron of musicians, and a symbol of harmony. With melodies from his magic instrument he has the power to make flowers grow and blossom immediately. Immortal Truong Qua Lao, a symbol of longevity, carries a bamboo tube and rod and watches over old men. Scholars and barbers are under the watchful eyes of Immortal La Dong Tan who carries a magic sword on his back, using it to slay harmful spirits and rid the world of evil. Actors have their patron in the figure of Immortal Tao Quoc Cuu. At the helm is Chief Immortal Han Chung Ly, a soldier and alchemist who has the power to transform himself. He is seen with a magic fan, symbolic of the delicacy of human feeling. With his fan he has the power to revive the souls of the dead. He is also a keeper of the Elixir of Life and, therefore, a symbol of longevity.

Embroidery on silk cloth featuring the Eight Immortals of Taoism, c. 1940 (77.5" x 37"). $1200.

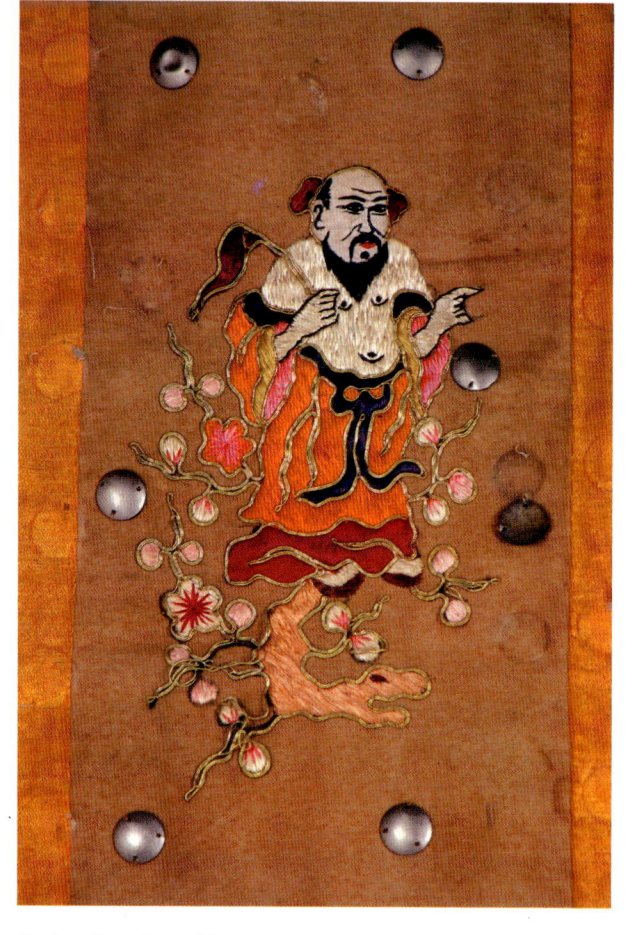

Detail of embroidery of Immortal Lam Thai Hoa, patron of florists.

Detail of embroidery of Immortal Ly Thiet Quai, protector of the ill and infirm.

Detail of embroidery of Immortal Ha Tien Co, who oversees the home, on the back of Phoenix.

Detail of embroidery of Immortal Han Tuong Tu, patron of musicians, on the back of Fish.

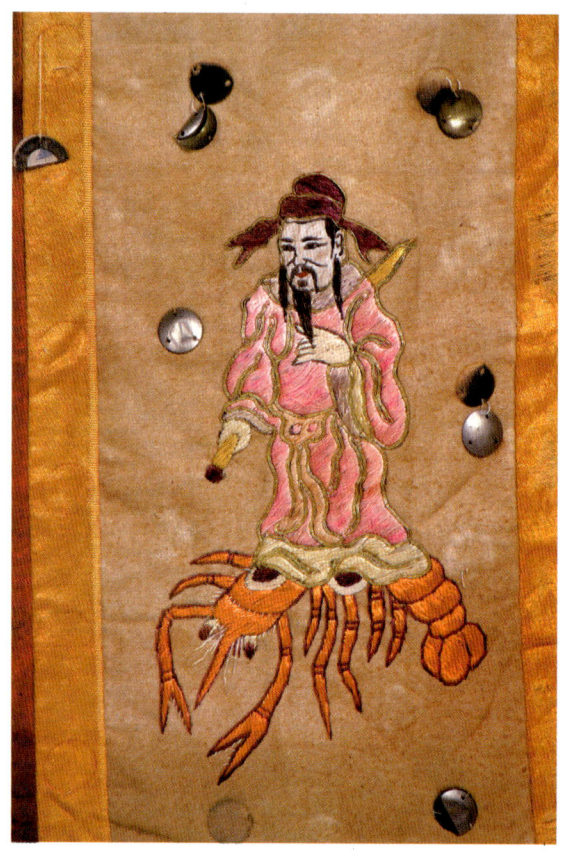

Detail of embroidery of Immortal Truong Qua Lao, protector of the old.

Detail of embroidery of Immortal La Dong Tan, opponent of evil, standing on a lobster.

142

Detail of embroidery of Immortal Tao Quoc Cuu, patron of actors, upon the back of Sacred Tortoise.

Detail of embroidery of Chief Immortal Han Chung Ly, able to prolong life, on the back of a crab.

143

The Eight Taoist Immortals embroidered on silk, c. 1900 (7.5" x 32"). $400.

Detail of two Immortals.

Lacquer panel with relief carved Immortals on sacred beasts, mother of pearl floral designs along the border, c. 1900 (35" x 13"). $1800/pair.

Detail of an Immortal holding a fan and upon Unicorn.

Detail of an Immortal upon Phoenix.

Immortals upon fabulous beasts.

145

Detail of a watercolor of a Taoist deity who oversees fathers and sons, c. 1940.

Glass painting of a benevolent guardian spirit who uses his sword to fight evil and stands atop a fabulous beast, c. 1950 (14" x 11.5"). $300.

Protective panel of The Eight Diagrams with Immortals, Dragons, and the creation symbol at the center, c. 1900 (9.8" x 11"). $350.

Confucianism

Confucianism arrived in Vietnam in 111 BC and stressed morality and keeping tradition. It has been a central guiding light in Vietnamese thought and life. It asserts common membership in an eternal cosmic order in which roles are ordained. For the sake of stability and order, these roles must be respected. As the universe itself is governed by a moral order, so should human behavior be moral. Stability, a sacred pursuit, requires that rulers follow a moral order and that the ruled, in turn, be respectful of and obedient to authority. If these principles are not followed, chaos and confusion will reign in place of stability and peace. It is a stringent code of ethics and it guided the behavior of all from royals to commoners, providing clear rules for their daily relationships. These ideas manifest themselves at the community level as obedience to civil authority and at the social level as obedience to parental authority, elders, teachers, the ancestors, and others.

Watercolor of two devotees giving homage before the altar, c. 1950. $350.

The Cao Dai

The Cao Dai faith is a very interesting and eccentric mixture of Taoism, Buddhism, Confucianism, popular cults, Christianity, and other world religions. It stresses service to others and the rejection of materialism. The faith came to Vietnam in 1926 and is estimated to have two million followers. Most devotees live in and around Tay Ninh. The most important aspect of its doctrine is a belief in a Supreme Being, or Cao Dai, who made his wishes known through teenage mediums. Most interesting, at least to outsiders, is the imagery of this religion. There are a wide range of saints including Confucius, Joan of Arc, Jesus Christ, and Victor Hugo. Also present are various others from Western history and culture who claimed to have had direct communication with God. These are clear examples of the mixed origins of this belief and the intent of its originators to give the religion a universal appeal by making the attempt to have a little of something for everyone.

Shamanism

Other beliefs include those among the ethnic people of Vietnam, for example, those residents from the Northeast. In this and other regions people may seek out the services of a shaman. He can provide guidance and advice in matters of the spirit world as he is considered to be literate and knowledgeable. In the eyes of believers, the shaman has a particular understanding of other realms and he possesses special powers to communicate with the world beyond earthly existence.

Provincial shaman's robe with embroidered horses and confronting Dragons, c. 1950 (36" x 23"). $750.

Reverse of robe with Dragon above a pair of Phoenixes and beneath dual moons.

Provincial shaman's robe with embroidered Dragons, horse, and Unicorn, c. 1950 (37.5" x 23.5"). $750.

Provincial shaman's robe with embroidered, confronting Dragons and Phoenix motifs, c. 1950 (35" x 27"). $750.

Reverse of robe, Dragon and Unicorn look skyward in the attitude of paying homage to the moon.

Reverse of robe with Dragon and horses.

149

Provincial shaman's robe rich with embroidery of Dragons, angels, and special objects, c. 1950 (40.5" x 36.5"). $1200.

Reverse of robe with a multitude of angels, animals, and special designs.

Detail of angels.

Detail of Sacred Unicorn.

150

Shaman's headdress embroidered with confronting Phoenixes who contend for a sacred object, c. 1950 (6" x 12.5"). $250.

Reverse side with contending serpent Dragons.

Christianity

Roman Catholicism was introduced into Vietnam in the 16th century by missionaries from France, Spain, and Portugal. Pope Alexander II assigned Vietnam its first bishops in 1659 and the first Vietnamese priests were ordained in 1665. Catholicism spread rapidly following the French conquest in the mid-19th century. The heaviest concentrations of Roman Catholics in Vietnam once were in the north, but many fled to the south after the partition of the country in 1954. Catholicism posed a set of thorny problems. First, the belief of God above the Emperor was alien and, secondly, it forbade the worship of false idols. Therefore, Catholics left their native villages and established new ones under the leadership of their parish priests. Often, the new villages existed side by side with the original village, but, if necessary, the priest led his parishioners into uncultivated areas and founded entirely new communities. Today, around ten percent of the population is Catholic and most Catholics live in Ninh Binh and Dong Nai Provinces.

There are a variety and range of religious beliefs in this nation. In Ho Chi Minh City, for example, one finds pagodas, temples, and mosques. Churches, Catholic and Protestant, are here. However, there is one constant, and that is the effect of traditional beliefs. Whatever the belief or faith, it has blended to a significant extent with ancient notions of a world of gods and spirits and it gives due homage to the role of the ancestors.

A Catholic church fashioned from metal and painted gold, c. 1920 (5" x 3.5" x 7"). $150.

A wood statue of Virgin Mary, her face and hands of carved ivory, c. 1900 (H 11"). $650.

An ivory carving of Virgin and Child, Virgin wears a silver crown topped by a pearl, c. 1900 (H 4.5"). $700.

Two altar vases symbolizing purity, c. 1920 (H 13"). $450/pair.

153

Chapter 14
Times Change

Notwithstanding the occasional notion that "they got it right the first time," the ultimate theme and truth revealed by any collection of vintage objects is the basic fact that times change, people move on, and the new replaces the old. Old items are sold, put away, neglected, and forgotten. There are younger, local collectors coming along and I believe this trend will continue. However, for the most part, collecting still remains a curiosity to locals who wonder why people spend money on things that are old and seemingly useless.

I see fewer and fewer of certain items as times move along. Soon, I suppose, many of these items will not be seen at all. Modernization and progress are taking their inevitable toll in Vietnam. The pace of life is changing and the aura of calmness evident in the Bat Trang porcelain figures may too become a thing of the past. The economic engine of Vietnam, Ho Chi Minh City, is moving full tilt towards big business and fancy shops with consumer goods of the kind seen in other major cities of the world. Dong Khoi Street, the former antiques center, is quickly becoming indistinguishable from other streets in other major modern cities as old gives way to new. The old shops I used to enjoy so much on this stretch have been replaced with boutiques and nice restaurants. Shopping malls, a kind of temple to modern society, are on the way. At warp speed, Vietnam weaves its way towards the future and relegates some vestiges of the past to the background.

And so it goes with the way of life they represent. It may be true, for example, that in the provinces many people still use oil lamps. But I imagine they would quite naturally prefer electricity and will quickly seize this resource when it becomes available. To continue with the example of the oil lamp, one can still find it being used in the cities as residents cope with frequent power outages though the wealthy will promptly turn on the generator to combat this inconvenience. The point is this: the oil lamp, like so many other things, will lose it grip and time will pass it by. The items here, like the oil lamp, are drifting into the past.

A shop sign advising patrons in Vietnamese, Chinese, and French that upstairs is for residence, not business, c. 1940 (13.5" x 11"). $100.

A documents box for the office, c. 1940 (16" x 16" x 17"). $350.

A provincial food box with inscriptions wishing health and happiness for the family, c. 1950 (D 9.5", H 8"). $200.

Bat Trang ceramic figure of an old, provincial home for a wealthy family, c. 1900 (H 3"). $300.

Bat Trang ceramic figure of mother and child, c. 1900 (H 3.5"). $300.

Bat Trang ceramic figure of a fisherman, c. 1900 (H 3.5"). $300.

Candle holder, probably for use on a boat or ship, c. 1940 (H 18"). $250.

An oil lamp of red colored glass, c. 1940 (H 18.5"). $250.

157

A pair of hook-shaped and copper oil lamps with flower petal tips, c. 1940 (H 11"). $300/pair.

A pair of oil lamps of colored glass, c. 1940 (D 3", H 6"). $250/pair.

158

A ceramic oil burner, c. 1900 (H 7"). $250.

A pair of bronze perfume burners, painted yellow, c. 1920 (H 5.5"). $250/pair.

Bibliography

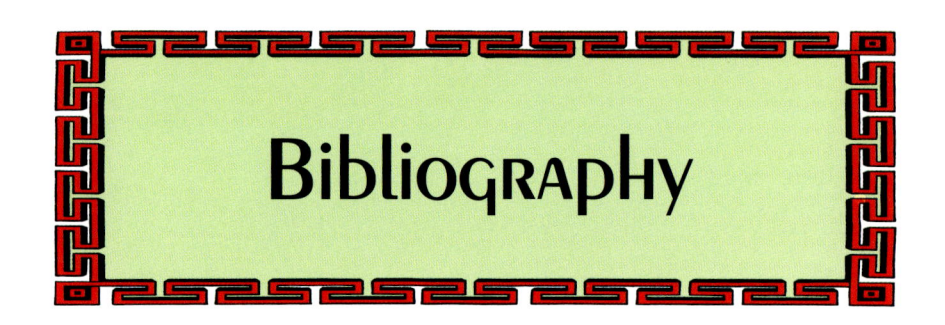

Bunag, Esperanza A. *The Tactile Appeal of Lacquer*. Orientations, Volume 5, Number 5, May 4, 1974, p. 35-44.

Cadiere, L. *L'Art a Hue*. Hue: L'Association des Amis du Vieux Hue, 1930.

Caddell, Ann C. *How Vietnamese Men Became Mandarins*, http://www.militaryliving.com/vietnam2/vietnamch5.htm

Diep, Trung Binh. *Patterns on Textiles of The Ethnic Groups in Northeast of Viet Nam*. Hanoi: Nha Xuat Ban My Thuat, 2003.

Freeman, Michael, Sian Evans, and Mimi Lipton. *In The Oriental Style: A Sourcebook of Decoration and Design*. London: Thames and Hudson Ltd, 1990 and 1996.

Friends of Vietnam Heritage, Hanoi Group. *Quan Thanh Temple*. Hanoi: The Gioi Publishing House, 2002.

Nguyen, Huyen V. *The Ancient Civilization of Vietnam*. Hanoi: The Gioi Publishing House, 1995.

Nguyen, Khac V. and Huy V. Le. *Arts and Handicrafts of Viet Nam*. Hanoi: The Gioi Publishing House, 1992.

Nguyen, Thong H. *Hue, Its Traditional Handicrafts and Trade Guilds*. Hue: Thuan Hoa Publishing House, 1994.

Pham, Thuong C. *But Thap Buddhist Art*. Hanoi: Fine Arts Publishing House, 1996.

Thai, Van Kiem. *Vietnamese Realities,* Sai Gon, 1969.

The Culture of Tea in Vietnam. http://1saigon.net/html/tea.htm

Tran, Hong D. and Ha Anh Thu. *A Brief Chronology of Vietnam's History*. Hanoi: The Gioi Publishing House, 2000.

Unger, Ann H. and Walter Unger. *Pagodas, Gods and Spirits of Vietnam*. London: Thames and Hudson, 1997.

Williams, C.A.S. *Outlines of Chinese Symbolism and Art Motives*. New York, New York: Dover Publications, Inc., 1976.